Communicating can help you to
Be Successful, Innovative, Extraordinary
In Business.

Managing Uncertainty

Be Successful, Innovative, Extraordinary, In Business.

How communicating can improve your business.

Brent Nelson Ph. D.

HH

Heather Hill

Cover Art BNelson

Table of Contents

Preface

Some businesses grow and become successful, while others stagnate and decline.

Some business adapt to change, while others become stuck in the past.

Some are a great place to work, while others have a high turnover.

So, what makes the difference?

All businesses face challenges, but what makes the difference depends on their version of social reality.

Social reality is what we do about the physical reality we encounter. In your business you encounter problems every day. So what do you do about them? How does your current social reality help or prevent you from being successful?

Communicating is how we create social reality.

Communicating is how we share our experiences and get to know other people. It is how we learn about ourselves, others, and the world around us. Understanding how communicating works is helpful to improving our quality of life

Communicating begins with one person and as the reader of this book that person is you. Developing communicating skills is important because of the amount of time we spend communicating.

It is how we gain information and new ideas.
It is how we learn to do things.
It is how we develop our identity and self-concept.
It is how we can help our career and promote personal growth.
It is how we support others and show that we care about them.
It is how we create and maintain relationships.
It is how we get to know ourselves, others, and the world around us.

This book was written to help you to increase your awareness, so you can have more options when you communicate with other people. However, there is no best approach that works for everyone all of the time. Only you can determine what works best for you.

This book can be used in businesses for education and training. It can be used in courses, seminars, or as a resource for schools, businesses, groups, and organizations. It is designed to be used with the companion communication skills book, *Be Smarter, Happier, Better-Looking.*

It covers many areas that can be helpful for people in business including communication skills, working with others, effective groups, relationships, self development, leadership, balancing work and family, and even how food can make everything better.

This book uses the words "communicating" or "communicate" instead of "communication" because communicating is an active process between people. It is written in a casual, conversational style for ease of reading with minimal technical terms.

This book utilizes scholarly research in new and creative ways for the purpose of reporting, commentary, analysis, and criticism to create new knowledge and insights. It is not meant to provide professional advice.

The author of this book is the first person to develop and apply new and innovative methodologies to understand how people are motivated by laws that govern communicating and behavior.

The author of this book is the first person to identify *The Nelsonian Laws of Uncertainty, Shared meaning, and Investing*, which comprise a *Grand Unified Theory of Behavioral Communication*. These laws have influenced communicating and behavior since the beginning of time.

Throughout history, most of human activity has been motivated by uncertainty. Yet, never before have so many people experienced so much uncertainty.

The last hundred and fifty years have seen more advancement in our quality of life than ever before. Society has made great advancements to reduce uncertainty, but it has likely made us more vulnerable to uncertainty.

Uncertainty affects all of us. It influences how we think and motivates our behavior. Understanding uncertainty can change how you think about practically everything.

It's helpful to understand how uncertainty affects you and your business, so you can be successful, innovative, and even extraordinary in business.

Chapter 1
Creating a Great Business

Imagine that you live in a rural farming community, so you have to grow all your own food to eat. For many years you have had good harvests. That is until last year. You barely got by and this year is shaping up to be even worse than the last.

If things don't change and it doesn't rain soon your crops will likely fail, and you will have nothing to eat. What do you do?

Depending on where you live and during which time period in history, you might pray more to atone for your sins. You might make animal sacrifices to the gods to improve your harvest. You might make human sacrifices. Or you might irrigate.

Throughout history all people have had one thing in common, they had to grow food to eat in order to survive. How they did that, and how they solved the problems they faced, depended on their version of social reality.

Social reality is what we do about the physical reality we encounter. In your business you encounter problems every day. So what do you do about them? How does your current social reality help or hurt you from being successful?

Do you do what you have done in the past or do you look for new solutions?

Social reality is important because it makes life predictable, society stable, and people happy. However, it can also constrain people making them shortsighted and causing them to fail. So how does your social reality help your business?

Everyone faces problems. It is what you do about them that makes a difference. Your particular version of social reality will determine what you do next. If it results in success or failure.

The Nature of Reality

Everything created by nature is governed by the laws of nature, like the laws of physics. Everything created by people has one thing in common, at one time it did not exist. It first existed as an idea in a person's mind who then had to make a connection to communicate their Great Idea to others, who had to understand it for it to become reality.

This process of developing and communicating our ideas to others works not only for the tangible things we create, but also for concepts and ideas. Often these ideas shape how people think and motivates their behavior creating physical reality. When people use this process to communicate their ideas to others, it helps to create social reality.

When we think of reality, we think of things like tangible objects that actually exist as opposed to something that exists in our mind. We don't necessarily consider concepts that exist in our mind as reality.

Communicating thoughts and ideas that exist in our mind can become as much of a reality as the tangible things all around us. What we think about and communicate to others can create a reality of its own.

Consider the following types of reality.

Physical reality.
Social reality.
Group reality.
Individual reality.

Physical reality.

Everything around us can be divided into two basic categories: everything created by nature and everything created by people. Physical reality includes everything that exists in nature including all living things and naturally occurring objects and phenomena. Some physical reality is created by people including things like houses, clothing, and furniture. When we invest physical reality with shared meaning, we create social reality.

Social reality.

Social reality is how we make sense of the world around us. It is created by people through the process of communicating with one another. Social reality reduces uncertainty because it provides the information, structure, and rules people need to function in society.

Social reality can create physical reality. While social reality exists in our minds, it can become as real as physical reality because of its power to motivate people's behavior. Social reality can determine what ideas are considered acceptable and how they should be implemented.

Social reality is how we interpret the information we gather creating our perspective of how we see ourselves, others, and the world around us. Often the events that happen to us and the things we see around us are open to different interpretations. Social reality tells us which interpretations are acceptable and which ones are not. It can determine how we react to events and what we do about them. It influences how we interpret our experiences and the experiences of others.

Social reality manifests itself in the tangible things people create. This can change over time affecting our physical reality. Even though people's needs have remained much the same throughout history, how they fulfilled them has changed considerably. We need to wear clothes, but the way we dress is determined by what social reality tells us is acceptable. It once motivated women to wear corsets and men to wear tights.

Social reality is created by people to reduce the uncertainty found in physical reality, so they can better understand the things that they perceive around them. It fulfills several needs including our need to create order out of chaos, our need to organize things around us, and our need for control. It tells us how we should act and what to do in various situations. It influences our behavior and keeps us in line with what is considered acceptable.

Social reality helps us to take the unfamiliar and make it familiar. It takes chaotic events and makes them understandable by giving them meaning so they can be useful to us. It is an important mechanism we utilize to deal with the unpredictable and chaotic events of life.

Social reality works because it fulfills many of our most fundamental needs including our need to know more about ourselves, others, and the world around us. It fulfills our need to exert control over our world by explaining how it works. It exerts control over people to create a stable society.

The power of social reality is in its ability to motivate behavior by altering how we interpret our physical reality. For example, at times people have interpreted the lack of rain that made for a poor harvest as God's displeasure with them. Some cultures responded to this physical reality with human sacrifices, others sacrificed animals, and others felt they needed to atone for their sins by praying more.

Today, we explain the lack of rain as being due to weather patterns, so we develop drought tolerant crops and build irrigation systems. In each of these societies, differing social realities explained the same physical reality in different ways motivating people to take different actions. This makes social reality very powerful because it motivates what people do about what they perceive.

Social reality helps bring our intangible thoughts and ideas into existence in physical reality. Everything created by people existed first in someone's mind who, through the process of communicating, shared it with others. As more people shared the idea it became a part of social reality. Even though social reality exists primarily in people's minds, it manifests itself in their behavior, actions, and how they communicate with others. Through their actions, it can create its own reality that can be as real as physical reality.

Group social reality.

Groups like a business can create their own specialized version of social reality by adding their ideas to meet their specific needs, wants, and desired outcomes. Group social reality often includes stories about how the group began, its founder, well known members, its history, significant events, and what it means to be a member.

It can develop slowly through people sharing meaning over time or be created intentionally in a comparatively short period of time. Some types of groups that develop their own specialized social reality include businesses, educational, religious, political, and cultural groups.

A group social reality is often created to fulfill the needs and wants of the group. It can be used to encourage commitment to the group. It may be communicated to the public in order to gain outside support or recruit new members. For most of these groups their shared group reality fits in with the larger social reality. Specific versions of social reality can be created by groups like political parties in order to promote a specific political agenda or to support candidates for public office.

Individual versions of social reality.

An individual social reality is how we as an individual organize and make sense of the world. Not everyone subscribes to every aspect of the larger societal social reality, nor do they have to in order to function in society. An individual's social reality can fall within the larger social reality, but can also deviate from it in certain aspects.

We may subscribe to part of it, but then alter or change other parts to fit our personal needs and wants. We do this because it helps us get through everyday life. Without it things would be more difficult. Since we created it, we can change it when it suits us.

However, like our self-concept, our individual reality develops slowly over time so that we may not even be aware of it. Our individual reality includes how we see ourselves, others, and the world around us. Awareness of this type of reality is important because of the influence it has on how we communicate and how it motivates our behavior.

At times different social realities can compete and even come in conflict with one another. This is because they may be based on different cultures, countries, religions, or political social realities that may not be compatible. Some people may belong to different groups that have conflicting social realities that can create confusion or tension. To resolve this tension we could develop our own version that combines elements from several other social realities.

Dramatic Narratives

When people come together, they often tell stories, but instead of giving an accounting of events, they may embellish what transpired. When people tell stories that have meaning to others, they may join in and share their own similar experiences. These stories can be emotional and might motivate people to take action.

Dramatic narratives often consist of a story about people or the retelling of events characterizing them from a particular point of view, giving them an emotional quality to make them more interesting or exciting. They are created to have a desired effect on people like informing, entertaining, or persuading them. So, they are invested with shared meaning by the people who create and share them.

When people share dramatic narratives they have the same understanding of events. Examining dramatic narratives can provide a way to understand the shared meanings embedded in what people say, as well as the underlying motives for their behavior. Much of how we understand reality is communicated through dramatic narratives because of their ability to reduce uncertainty.

When people communicate, they talk about themselves often telling stories about their past experiences. When they do, they might edit these stories to make them more interesting and exciting to the listener. When people understand and relate to these stories, they share meaning. This creates a connection, so they feel that they have something in common. This can make people seem more likable, even creating feelings of empathy.

The process of sharing meaning deals with the human tendency to want to understand other people to reduce uncertainty about them. Shared meaning is how a person makes a connection with other people, so that they see things in a similar way. This is how a group or organization gains and maintains people's support.

In dramatic narratives, real events are explained to create and maintain shared meaning with other people and to support a specific version of social reality. Much social reality is constructed through dramatic narratives. They are often given a dramatic, persuasive, or emotional quality to make them more interesting and attractive. This helps people to better understand them.

Dramatic narratives can include heroes and villains, along with characterizations of their actions as being good or bad. A person might cast themselves in their own dramatic narratives as the hero who will save the people from a villain who is out to destroy everything they hold dear.

Over time, many dramatic narratives can form a recognizable and meaningful view of society that helps to create social reality. The power of social reality lies in its ability to explain our experiences and the world around us reducing uncertainty. It can be used to explain the motivation for people's behavior.

The sharing of social reality is a way of creating a common understanding of the world and how it works. The shared meaning contained in dramatic narratives can create a social reality for people. Even though it may or may not accurately reflect actual physical reality, it may be no less real for them. The creation of social reality is motivated by people's need to reduce uncertainty by explaining events in order to make sense of them.

Social reality is created because people want to reduce uncertainty. They want to know about the world around them and social reality can be used to explain and predict physical reality. People often prefer a reality they have created themselves, because they are more comfortable in a world made up of familiar elements.

For instance, employees want to know what they can expect from their employer and what their employer expects from them. This is often explained through social reality. This means that social reality can be as important to people as physical reality because much of human interaction is socially constructed.

Social reality can be powerful because it tells people how to interpret physical reality and what to do about it. It can be used to explain events by telling people what is happening to them and how they fit in. It tells them what behaviors are accepted and which ones are not. It can serve as a comprehensive explanation of how things work in society. It can also facilitate confidence in a business and its leaders by reducing uncertainty about them.

Social reality has a larger, more important function, it can influence who we are as an individual and what kind of person we want to be. It can determine who we are as a group of people and what kind of business we want to be.

At one time our social institutions were only an idea shared by people. It was their vision of what they should be that shaped the world we live in today. It is the shared meanings we have today that will determine what kind of world future generations will live in tomorrow.

Organizations

We spend a lot of our time in organizations like businesses because they make significant contributions to society and the lives of the people who are a part of them. An organization is a group of people brought together by common interests to achieve mutual desired outcomes. They can create their own specialized form of social reality affecting how they see themselves, others, and the world around them.

We are motivated to join them because they have the ability to allocate resources to help us achieve our desired outcomes and fulfill material and social needs and wants. This gives them power to motivate and influence behavior. In many ways groups and organizations can have considerable influence over us.

Organizations are often made up of many smaller groups joined by connections making up networks that regulate the flow of information and resources. They tend to be more formal than groups with well defined rules, structures, and boundaries. They have tasks and desired outcomes that members are expected to fulfill based upon specialized roles.

Organizations centralize power with clear lines of authority, levels of management, and a hierarchy of importance. They allocate resources, provide benefits, and extract costs giving them power over their members. They have norms of behavior that are regulated by rules enforced with rewards and punishments.

There are many different types of organizations, so for the purpose of this book the word organization can refer to many kinds of entities including, but not limited to businesses, corporations, not for profit groups, government, schools, religious institutions, social clubs, and community groups.

We create organizations like businesses because they have the ability to reduce uncertainty in ways that individuals and groups cannot do. They can do this because they have the ability to gather and allocate resources for their members.

Organizations can make us feel more safe and secure by reducing uncertainty. They reduce uncertainty by creating structure, so everyone knows what is expected of them and what they can expect of others.

By working together with others, we can accomplish tasks that we could not accomplish working alone. They have longevity, the ability to continue to exist long after the founders and current members are gone, increasing stability and predictability for their members. They reduce uncertainty by fulfilling material, social, status, and security needs making them attractive to join.

Organizations are held together by the connections between members that form networks through which they share meaning. Members share meaning about the organization including its history, how it was founded, its values, and common purpose. They share meaning about what it means to be a member of the organization.

An organization can work like a marketplace where communicating is the currency and people are constantly making offers that are being accepted or rejected.

Understanding organizational behavior and how its members communicate with one another can work rather like a balance sheet that can be utilized to analyze the effectiveness of an organization.

This can measure how willing people are to invest in an organization and each other, and how much of a return they expect on their investment. The difference between an individual's perceptions and expectations can be an indicator of their commitment. The degree to which their needs and wants are being met can be an indicator of their satisfaction or dissatisfaction, which can affect their commitment to the organization.

An organization can be like an individual with its own needs and wants that must be fulfilled in order to function. It exists for a reason and its members must accomplish tasks to achieve its desired outcomes. If they don't, the organization will not function and might cease to exist.

An organization is created by the connections between people, so no one has total control over it. It is a separate entity from the people who comprise it because they create it between them. While members contribute to its existence, it can take on a life of its own with its own personality.

Individual members have their own needs and wants that motivate them to join an organization. Organizations are attractive because they can fulfill many of these needs and wants.

They fulfill not only monetary needs, but also the need for inclusion, status, respect, self-esteem, growth, and a feeling of contributing something worthwhile to make a difference.

Tension can be created between the needs and wants of the organization and the individual members. However, individuals must put the organization's needs first in order for the organization to function effectively.

Organizations can create their own specialized version of social reality that can regulate individual members' behavior. An organization often has its own social reality, which can include its history, how it was founded, and why it exists.

People may share stories about the founders including what kind of people they are, and their achievements. While these stories are based upon fact, there is often an element of drama added to make them more exciting.

These stories are more than just reminiscences of the past, they have a message for members about the organization. They communicate organizational expectations about its values and how members should behave. Sharing these stories is motivated by the law of shared meaning because it creates a connection that brings members together for a common purpose.

For example, people tell stories about the history of the United States including historical figures like George Washington and Thomas Jefferson. These stories have a message beyond a recollection of events, they communicate a deeper message of communal values and beliefs. They are used to share social reality like what America stands for and what it means to be an American.

Organizational satisfaction.

Everyone has perceptions and expectations about themselves, others, and the organization. They have expectations about what they are supposed to contribute and receive. They have perceptions about how well those expectations are being met, which may or may not reflect reality.

People often have differing perceptions and expectations that can make them feel satisfied or dissatisfied about their role in the organization. Satisfaction helps to increase a member's commitment encouraging them to do their job more effectively. Dissatisfaction can decrease commitment making people unhappy, perhaps even motivating them to leave.

Satisfaction is an emotional response to a person's perception of the difference between what they are contributing to an organization compared to what they are receiving from it based on their expectations. Everyone's expectations are different because they are based on past experiences, comparisons to others, and their self-concept. When people perceive that they are receiving fair rewards for fair work they are more likely to be satisfied.

When they feel they are contributing, but not receiving fair rewards, they can become dissatisfied. This means that member satisfaction is often based upon their perception of how well their needs and wants are being fulfilled, which may or may not reflect reality.

Generally, the higher degree of satisfaction the more a person is motivated to commit to the organization by contributing their time and resources. The law of investing motivates people to reduce or withdraw their commitment in an organization when they feel they are not getting fair rewards.

This is why it can be helpful to understand how member satisfaction works because when members are dissatisfied, it can undermine the effectiveness of the organization. This can reduce their commitment motivating them to withdraw resources and perhaps even leave. While there will always be some dissatisfaction in any organization, if the level becomes too great it may no longer be able to function effectively.

Organizational growth.

Organizations like a business often start out small and when it becomes successful, it attracts other people and grows larger. When it gets too large to function as a group, it may divide into two or more groups creating the need for an organizational structure to keep it together.

When a business grows so large that everyone cannot communicate directly, like face to face, with everyone else, it needs to develop structures so it can function.

This increases a business's needs and wants requiring more people to fulfill them. As a business grows, the nature of the tasks shift from the original purpose for which it was created to organizing the business. For example, a person starts a store that is successful, so it expands to other locations. As it grows, the focus shifts from selling things to managing store locations and employees.

People are no longer hired just to sell things in the store, but also to run the organization doing managerial tasks such as accounting, inventory, human resources, and property management. These tasks must now be accomplished, so the business can function before anything is actually sold.

In a small business, one person may fulfill many roles and do multiple tasks giving them more experience and developing more skills. They can get a broader view of the organization, what it does, and how everything works together.

As a business get larger, more tasks need to be done so more people are needed to do them. This can lead to role specialization where people devote more of their time to a specific task concentrating on a particular task or skill.

In larger businesses many people may be assigned to a specific task. This can unintentionally create boundaries, so employees may not understand how everything fits together or how the overall organization works.

They may no longer feel that they contribute or they may not know how what they do fits into the big picture because they only communicate with people close to them, who do what they do and not with people in other areas of the business. This can make the business lose focus that could fracture it because fewer people know how everything works together.

People can have a feeling of accomplishment when they know how what they do helps the business. It can be helpful to have a way for people to move around doing different tasks to gain more skills.

This benefits everyone because they can do many tasks increasing their flexibility rather than specializing where they can do just a few. They know how things work together giving them the big picture. This can help facilitate professional growth increasing their satisfaction and commitment. They also gain the ability to know how the business works, which can help them to become leaders.

Organizational structure.

In order to function effectively, organizations need structure including rules, roles, and norms of behavior. Structure usually consist of different types of connections between members. Organizations need to develop stable structures, so that they can accomplish their tasks and achieve their desired outcomes.

Structure can be defined by the boundaries that exist in and around the organization. Organizational structure should be clearly communicated, so all members understand what is expected of them and what they can expect of others. How an organization structures itself can bring people together or it can divide them by pushing them apart.

Rules are how an organization implements its version of social reality. Most organizations have their own set of formal and informal rules. Formal rules are often written down in handbooks, guidelines, contracts, and other written documents. Their purpose is to regulate individual behavior by conforming to the norms and expectations of the organization to help it to accomplish its tasks.

In addition to the formal organizational rules, groups within the organization often create their own set of informal rules. These rules are rarely written down, but can be more effective in regulating the behavior of its members. They are often created by the members through the process of behavioral reinforcement.

Most of the time we only learn about these rules after they have been broken and we are reprimanded. We can learn the rules by observing the behavior of others or asking a more experienced member.

Organizational space.

Space consists of everything that is around us. There are many types of space and there are many ways that we utilize it. We have the physical spaces we occupy like where we live and work, including our homes and workplaces. We create emotional space in relationships with others. We have space that we seek to control such as areas of influence and expertise like our turf or territory. How we use space can communicate information about ourselves to others.

When we invest spaces with meaning it gives them value. We invest our time, energy, effort, and money in them to make them more useful or attractive to us. The more we spend time in a space, the more we invest ourselves in it, so the more we feel connected to it.

We define our space by establishing boundaries. We use boundaries in practically every area that we use space including physical, emotional, psychological, and relational. We use walls to create physical boundaries. We take time for ourselves to create emotional boundaries. We have responsibilities defined by psychological boundaries. We create rules in relationships that serve as relational boundaries. We do this to reduce uncertainty by exerting control over areas that we feel are ours.

For instance, we give our physical spaces like our workplace or office a sense of identity by filling it with our personal items as an extension of our own self-concept. This is why if we perceive that others invade our territory we might take action to defend it because we perceive it as an intrusion on who we are.

The spaces we occupy at work communicate our status, importance, and position. In organizations there are some spaces that are more prestigious than others and the competition for them invests them with meaning, which gives them value. When spaces are valued by people they can be used as a reward for achievement.

How space is arranged can influence our behavior. We are more likely to talk with someone at a nearby desk then someone a long distance away. People use space to put barriers between themselves and others, which can create a perception of having status.

We like to personalize our workspaces by displaying things like artwork, books, plants, or photographs to make it an extension of ourselves that reflects our personality. This communicates information about ourselves as well as letting others know that it is our space.

We do this to reduce uncertainty for ourselves by making our space feel more familiar and comfortable. It makes our work more enjoyable helping us to be more productive. We tend to work better and get more done when we are in a space that we find enjoyable. It gives us a sense of pride in ownership encouraging our commitment to the organization.

Organizational climate.

Organizational climate describes the nature of how people communicate with one another. It is important because it can affect people's state of mind. While it is mostly psychological in nature, it is communicated through the social interaction of people, so it can have tangible results manifested in their behavior.

Climate is an important part of an organization because it can make us feel good about ourselves. A positive climate makes an organization a fun place to be, motivating people to want to be a part of it. A negative climate can reduce an individual's commitment to the organization, so they feel less satisfied, making them more likely to leave.

Organizational climate is important because it affects the ability of people to work together. People can pick up on the emotional intensity of others and transfer their emotions through the connections between individuals that comprise a business's communicating networks.

Organizational climate includes the degree of openness people feel when they communicate with each other. They may share information freely, openly, and honestly. Conversely, a climate may be restrictive so people don't say what's on their mind.

A business has degrees of adaptability that can vary between strict and flexible. Some have strict standards that people are expected to comply with giving them little individual choice. This is likely to occur when the task is specific like a sports team where the desired outcome is to win.

Others are more flexible so individual choice and creativity are important. Each organization has to find a balance between strict and flexible that helps them accomplish their desired outcomes.

In organizations people tend to follow familiar patterns of communicating. These are the reoccurring patterns we use to talk with one another. These patterns can create climates that are positive or negative, warm or cold, and friendly or formal.

The climate in an organization can often be characterized like the weather. It may be sunny, cloudy, or stormy. It can be hot or cold, depending upon people's emotional levels. Positive climates can be characterized as warm and sunny, and negative ones can be cold and stormy.

These climates can travel through an organization like storms travel across the countryside. Sometimes you can do something to improve them. Other times, just like the weather, there's not much you can do other than taking cover and riding them out until they pass.

Since climate is comprised of the social atmosphere within an organization, it is open to people's perceptions that may or may not be accurate. If people perceive others are feeling a certain way they may be more inclined to think that they should feel the same way too.

People have expectations about what type of climate they need to do their best work. This is often based upon their past experiences and personal preferences. Some people prefer a climate that is informal, fun, warm, friendly, and open to new ideas and information. Others may prefer a more fixed, formal, and structured climate that values tradition.

People have expectations about the climate in which they work. They may expect the organization to be open and flexible or closed and strict. If people fit in with the organizational climate, they are more likely to feel comfortable as a part of the organization. If the climate is meeting their needs, it can increase their satisfaction and commitment.

If a person does not fit in with the organizational climate they can feel uncomfortable, not accepted, or that their needs are not being met. They may feel like an outsider. This can create tension undermining the effectiveness of the organization.

An organization's climate can have a great influence on people's self-concept, which can affect their satisfaction and commitment to the group. If a climate is cold, formal, or overly negative it can hurt people's self-concept because it is affected by reflected feedback through the process of communicating.

Negative climates can develop without people being aware of them. Increasing your awareness can help to keep the climate from becoming too negative and make it more positive and productive. People may be communicating negative messages for a reason, so it can be helpful to understand why they do it.

By looking for more information and asking questions, the emotional intensity can be reduced to help make a negative climate more positive. Having an awareness of how climates affect us can help us to not fall into these patterns.

Organizational culture.

Organizational culture consists of the reoccurring patterns of communicating and behavior that comprise a specialized method of interaction between individuals within an organization. This can help the organization to be more effective because it reduces uncertainty by providing structure and stability.

The culture of an organization serves a similar function as the culture of a country or geographic region. It can communicate its history, language, customs, rituals, and social reality. This can make becoming a new member of an organization feel like going to a foreign country. It's helpful for members of an organization to know its culture to increase their satisfaction and commitment to it.

While organizational climate can change to reflect the emotional intensity of the moment, organizational culture changes more slowly. The culture often begins when an organization is created and develops in one of two ways. It can grow spontaneously through the natural interaction of its members over time through the process of behavioral reinforcement.

Or, it can be created and developed intentionally to achieve specific desired outcomes. However, when a culture is imposed on an organization the members may try to create their own informal culture. By understanding how culture works, organizations can develop a culture that is the most effective for them.

Communicating with members and customers improves the effectiveness of the organization. This can make courtesy an important part of an organization's culture because it affects how members communicate with each other and the public.

Courtesy is more than just being polite or having good manners, it is an attitude that people have towards one another. Courtesy can motivate behavior because people are encouraged to be thoughtful and considerate, and show respect for others.

There is a culture of civility and graciousness. It encourages an organizational climate that is cordial, warm, and friendly making it a pleasant place to work, that can increase satisfaction and commitment.

Organizational rituals and traditions.

An important part of how we develop culture is through rituals and traditions. Rituals are established patterns of communicating or behavior repeated in a similar way over time. They might involve the ways in which members interact and communicate with one another. They may involve regularly occurring activities such as coffee breaks or Monday morning meetings.

Traditions are patterns of behavior that a members share based upon their mutual customs or beliefs. For example, an organization may believe strongly in supporting the families of its members, so they have events in which family members are encouraged to participate. Organizations often have rites of passage like a party or ceremony when a person gets promoted, changes departments, or retires.

These activities reduce uncertainty because members get to know one another on a more personal level. When members participate in rituals and traditions together, it gives them a sense of unity of purpose and a feeling that everyone is in it together. This can be helpful in larger organizations where all members cannot feasibly get together at the same time. By participating in the same events, they are part of the same community.

Organizational self-replication.

Have you ever noticed that some organizations don't ever seem to change, even over long periods of time? For example, you may have noticed a business or government agency that seems to have the same people working there even though it is many, many years later.

They act, talk, perhaps even look the same. You may have even thought they were the same people at first, but after so many years that could not be possible.

This could be a business where you worked, a store where you shopped, or a government office. If it has happened to you it can be a strange phenomenon to experience and there is a good reason for it.

In many organizations there can be an internal inertia that resists change. This can be propagated by a self-replicating mechanism that works rather like cells in the human body. Our body replaces old cells with new ones that look the same as those they replace. If they were too different, our appearance would change and we would look different.

People leave organizations and have to be replaced with new people. The people who select their replacements often self-replicate by hiring people like those who left or who are like themselves. Uncertainty motivates them to hire and promote people who are similar to those already in the organization. They hire them to reduce uncertainty because it promotes stability and security.

An organization is like other living organisms, it seeks to eliminate what it perceives as a threat. If new members are too different they could increase uncertainty that may pose a threat to the existing members. Existing members may be reluctant to accept people they perceive as being too different, because if the new people think too differently, they could challenge the existing members' social reality creating tension.

If the new person's way of thinking prevails, the existing members might be perceived as being wrong undermining their power and authority potentially damaging their self-concept. This can provide motivation for organizations to avoid implementing change. This can be one reason why organizations can grow to a point where they cease to innovate and begin to stagnate, or decline.

If the new members are too different than the existing members they may not fit in and could be ostracized, even rejected by the existing members. New members may feel pressure to change their behavior to fit in with the organization and its culture. If they do not change, it could hurt their self-concept making them become dissatisfied and frustrated with the organization, so they may eventually leave.

Organizations need new people and new ideas. What worked in the past may no longer work today. The old ways need to be challenged. and new ways tested. If everyone thinks the same, this will not happen and the organization will stagnate or decline. The members may not even be aware they have a problem. They can have an attitude of, we know what we are doing, we've done this for years.

Organizational growth and decline.

A business goes through developmental phases because they are created by the connections between people. They can go through a process of creation, growth, maintenance, and decline. They can become successful and grow until they reach a point where the business reaches a plateau, so growth and innovation declines or even ends and it goes out of business.

So, how can a business be innovative and creative, grow successful, only to decline and wither away? This process can be described by three phases of organizational development, which begins with the uncertainty phase.

When a business is first created there's a high degree of uncertainty. Uncertainty can work as a motivational influence if it is managed effectively. The people who comprise it are learning how to negotiate their roles, norms, rules, structure, and social reality. They go through the process of behavioral reinforcement trying different things until they are accepted by others.

At this point, there is a high degree of uncertainty, so they are likely the most open they can be to new ideas and new ways of doing things. This flexibility helps them to be innovative and creative.

When a business becomes larger and older, chances are good that they have significantly reduced uncertainty. They have solidified their roles, norms, rules, structure, and social reality. Rather than negotiating these things, members are now expected to conform to the business's ways of doing things.

People with different ideas may be cast as troublemakers to be ignored or removed. Reduced uncertainty provides security and stability, however, it also reduces flexibility and the ability to adapt to change. This can create an attitude of, "I know what I'm doing," which can lead to arrogance. Arrogance can be one of the leading causes of organizational decline.

Reduced uncertainty is followed by the shared meaning phase of development. As most of the people are new, they're involved in the process of sharing meaning about themselves, others, and the business. They negotiate between themselves what the business stands for and what it means to be a part of it.

Since this is a fluid process, it's open to change and interpretation. As a business grows and becomes larger, it has more established shared meanings about the business and what it means to be a member. Members have less ability to contribute to change that meaning, and are instead expected to conform to it. People who share different meanings about the business are more likely to change to fit in or leave.

When a business is new, people usually have very little invested in it because the business has not yet developed. It is less likely to have established much structure or hierarchies that can create value in a business.

This means that people are more flexible and willing to try different approaches to become effective and successful because there is less investment to lose. Structure is developed to help increase stability, but it can also restrict innovation and trying new things that could be successful.

When a business goes through the investing phase of development, people can become more cautious about what they do because they do not want to loose the time, energy, and other resources they have invested in it.

This can make them less likely to innovate or do things differently because doing so could be perceived as increasing uncertainty. There are often hierarchies and ranks created by people because they have invested significant amounts of their time there. They are likely to resist change and innovation because they do not want to risk losing their investment, future benefits, or their place in the business.

The process of communicating will change as a business grows larger. In the beginning, it is generally smaller so people can communicate with everyone in the business more frequently regardless of rank. Information at the bottom can more easily flow to the top where decisions are made.

There's less apprehension about communicating across the business because it is smaller and everybody is closer, physically as well as psychologically. It is more likely that everyone is all in one location sharing the same physical space. This encourages communicating networks to facilitate the flow of information needed to innovate and grow.

In a larger business, people are often less likely to communicate across the organization because it is more difficult and can be perceived as increasing uncertainty. A business's culture may even discourage it. Instead, there are often established formal communicating networks people are expected to use.

People can be more distant, often physically separated by offices, different floors, perhaps even different locations. They may be reluctant to share their ideas for fear of rejection, punishment, or the loss of their investment.

People are more likely to communicate with others on the same level or in the same department. This can reduce the flow of information that could help them be innovative and creative, by reducing their awareness leading to poorer decisions. This can encourage some to use information as a means to improve their own position rather than the organization.

A business has its own needs and wants, just as individuals do. When a business is starting out it has lots of needs and wants, but it likely has few resources to fulfill them. This can motivate people to do more with less. It encourages them to come up with new and creative ways of doing things in order to save resources like time and money. When a business gets larger, it can have more resources, but there still is a problem of allocation.

In order to receive the resources they need, people are more likely to conform to the expectations of those that provide the resources, rather than developing their own means of accomplishing a task. They are more likely to be less innovative and creative. They can be less likely to question their superiors and just do what they're told.

When a business is new, people utilize the social reality of society or their past experiences. They may share different social realities that can create uncertainty about the business and what to expect. As it grows, people negotiate what the social reality of the business will eventually become.

This means that to some extent they have a say in what the business will look like, how it behaves, how it communicates, and what it does. This can provide more flexibility to create a business that is highly receptive not only to its employees, but also to its customers and the outside environment.

As a business grows, its social reality solidifies, so people have less say in what that means. It can also become more resistant to outside influences. It could develop a culture where it not only does not accommodate change, it actually resists it. This can make a business less flexible in responding to changing circumstances necessary for it to function effectively.

A business does not have to fall into this pattern of growth, stagnation, and decline. By having an awareness of this process and its causes, it can take measures to prevent it. This can happen in two ways.

First, it can happen at the very beginning when a business is formed. It can happen when people are negotiating how it will function. They can provide a mechanism for the group to bring in new information facilitating change.

This needs to be part of its culture. While this is probably the easiest way to do this, it takes an understanding of the process and the foresight to do it in order to instill it into a business from the beginning.

The second approach is to develop a new culture after a business has existed for some time. This is more common, however, once a business develops its culture, it can be difficult to change. Change has to begin at the very top and permeate all levels throughout a business. The new culture should encourage communicating across all levels and with people outside a business, like customers.

This facilitates new ideas and innovation, so people feel safe trying new things that could help the business without the fear of being penalized or losing their investment. The new culture has to be clearly communicated to everyone in the business. There also needs to be a means to work with those who might resist change so they don't see it as a threat to their position, power, or investment in the business.

Organizational change.

While the larger social reality must change, once we adopt a particular social reality it may be difficult to change because it provides us with stability and security. We might react negatively to others who try to change it because change represents increased uncertainty. This is because social reality becomes a part of who we are and our self-concept, so we may see attempts to change it as threatening.

We may resist change because if one part of what we believe is wrong, other things we believe could potentially be wrong as well. This can make us feel uncomfortable because it could undermine our feelings of safety and security increasing uncertainty. This motivates people to defend their version of social reality.

Change is inevitable and unavoidable because if social reality never changed we would still think the earth was flat and the sun revolved around the earth. In the past, people have resolved the tension created by conflicting social realities through various means including violence, war, and revolution.

For example, the American Revolutionary War was about more than independence from England. It was to legitimize the changing social reality about the nature of self-determination in government.

Having the ability to create a mechanism that allows social reality to adapt and change is essential to growth. Maintaining a constant social reality may be comfortable, however, without change to reflect changing needs and wants it would be nearly impossible for us to function in a constantly changing world.

While social reality governs how society works, in order for society to develop it needs a mechanism that allows for change while maintaining stability. One way this happens is through creative expression. Some groups and individuals such as artists, writers, fashion designers, actors, and musicians differentiate from accepted social reality by creating a specialized individual or group social reality.

This allows new ideas like artistic tastes and fashion trends to be tested and accepted before they become part of the larger social reality. For instance, there was a time when rock music and impressionistic painting were considered scandalous, but today they are considered part of our culture. This mechanism allows for new shared meaning to be created without excessively increasing uncertainty.

Organizational change is part of the process of how we restore economic equilibrium in groups, organizations, and even in society. One of the functions of organizations is to reduce uncertainty to create stability over long periods of time. However, since change is inevitable, organizations need a means to change without creating tension between change and stability.

People may say that they want change because they do not want to be perceived as being old fashioned or close minded, while at the same time they might resist it by saying things like, "That's the way we've always done things around here."

Organizational self-replication can perpetuate a static culture that resists change because it is perceived as uncomfortable increasing uncertainty. Change takes leadership and a willingness to change, but change should not be done just for its own sake. Even if people want change, actually getting them to change can be difficult. So, organizations may need to develop a means to reduce uncertainty to maintain stability while bringing in new ideas that can facilitate change.

People are more likely to change when uncertainty makes them uncomfortable. If change is portrayed as a means to reduce uncertainty to make things more stable and secure, uncertainty about change is reduced, so people are more likely to accept it. People are more likely to accept change when it is based on past traditions based upon common values and beliefs.

People may object to change for fear of losing the investment they have in the organization. So, it's helpful to reassure them that their investment will not be lost, but will likely increase. They are more likely to support change if they feel their investment today will payoff with greater returns tomorrow.

People are more likely to accept small changes over time. There is a threshold for change that people are willing to accept. After that, uncertainty increases to the point that they are motivated to resist it. If the change is below that level, they are less likely to pay as much attention to it.

People who are respected or held in high esteem can use their influence to convince others to change. Have people participate in the process because they will be more likely to support change that they feel they had a say in creating. They join organizations to have their needs and wants fulfilled, so present change as a means to better fulfill them.

Change can benefit everyone if they are aware of what is happening and have a say in what it will become.

Social Reality

Examining how uncertainty drives innovation and creativity can help us understand how to improve society and our quality of life. The process of communicating can be applied to examining the means by which people's ideas become physical reality.

Discovery and innovation is facilitated by the social reality we share because there first has to be the right conditions to encourage people to think differently about things and then communicate their Great Idea to others. Innovation encourages people to develop new ideas and new ways of doing things to make them a reality.

Throughout history, changes in social reality have changed the nature of society. In the Middle Ages, social reality was based on The Church and religious texts of the past. This social reality was changed by The Reformation and The Renaissance.

Changes in social reality allowed the introduction of the scientific method, which created new knowledge through research. This resulted in changes in physical reality that were so useful in advancing society they are still utilized today.

When an idea is communicated and accepted it is more likely to become a reality. This makes the conceptual process that precedes the creation of physical reality especially important. How information like your Great Idea is communicated through connections between people can determine how it can manifest itself in physical reality.

Advancements in society are motivated by uncertainty because it makes people look beyond what they already know to understand what they don't know.

Chapter 2
The Theory of Everything

What if you found yourself in a place that was unfamiliar to you, that you knew nothing about?

What if you were surrounded by people you did not know, who you could not communicate with or understand? What would you do?

While this is unlikely to happen, it is similar to what we experience when we are born. When we are born, we are surrounded by people we cannot clearly communicate with or understand. We are totally dependent upon them for all of our needs to live.

This motivates us to start a lifelong process of developing communicating skills, so we can better understand ourselves, others, and the world around us.

At some time in the distant past, humans began to explore a planet they knew little about. They encountered things and had experiences they sought to understand.

They experienced a high degree of uncertainty that motivated them to try to reduce it in order to fulfill their needs and wants. So, they had to develop ways of communicating with one another to better understand themselves, other people, and the world around them.

This process of gaining understanding through communicating has worked over time to advance human society. Practically everything we do, everything we think, everything we learn, everything we experience, and everything we know is created and shared by communicating with other people.

The history of human civilization is the process of gaining and sharing a better understanding of ourselves, others, and the world around us in order to reduce uncertainty.

This book is about the process by which we learn about ourselves, others, and the world around us. It is about how our needs and wants motivate us to communicate with others. It is about how we share our experiences to create meaning. It is about how uncertainty has motivated practically all of human activity throughout history.

Needs and wants.

Uncertainty begins with how we were created. As human beings we are all born with needs we cannot fulfill ourselves. They must be fulfilled by others so that we can survive. From the time we are born, we try to communicate our needs to others who try to understand them. Having needs that must be fulfilled motivates a lifelong process of communicating with others.

We can have virtually unlimited wants that are constrained by limited resources. We can feel tension between competing needs because we may not have the resources to fulfill them. We have needs and wants that we cannot fulfill ourselves, so we are motivated to communicate with others to fulfill them.

We have many needs that can be grouped into the following types.

Physical needs include everything we need to survive such as air, food, water, clothing, and shelter. Physical needs are universal because everyone needs to have them fulfilled.

We have material needs including making money. Material needs also include the things we have that make everyday life possible. It seems that when people have some needs or wants fulfilled, they may feel the need for more. They want new and better things. People can have virtually unlimited needs and wants, which can be restrained by limited resources.

We have spiritual needs like the need to know more about ourselves such as who we are, where we came from, and where we are going. We need to know more about God and why we were created. We need to feel connected to others, cared for, supported, and to support others. We need to learn about ourselves, others, and the world around us.

We need to feel a sense of accomplishment, to feel useful and that what we do matters. We want to be part of a group and have connections with other people. We need to be included, feel accepted by others, and that we fit in. We want to be liked and be loved. We want to care about others and have them care about us.

We need to have relationships, but we also need our own space. We feel the need to work, but we also need rest. We need enjoyment, pleasure, entertainment, fun, and to escape by getting away from our daily routines. We want others to have a positive image of ourselves. We want to have prestige, status, respect, or to be well regarded. When we fulfill these needs, we feel valued.

People need to have some control over their life. They may use control as a type of emotional release. When they become upset they may clean the house or rearrange the furniture to fulfill a need to control something in their lives.

We have a need for self-expression by discovering who you truly are. By knowing yourself and being able to communicate that to others. We want to be all we can be, fulfill our destiny, develop our talents, or following our calling. Self-fulfillment is not about what you do, it's about how you do it. It comes from doing what you enjoy to the best of your ability.

Which of these needs we have depends on each individual person. Some people need to be around others, while others need time to themselves. We choose the ones that are important to fulfill and which ones are not.

By being aware of how our needs and wants motivate our behavior and how we communicate with others, we can make choices about what we do rather than re-acting to things without knowing why.

We may feel frustration, depression, or tension in our lives and wonder why we are feeling this way. We often have more needs and wants than we have resources to fulfill, forcing us to set priorities that can be difficult because it leaves some of them unfulfilled creating tension.

Some needs and wants are mutually exclusive and cannot be fulfilled at the same time creating tension between them. For example, if our family wants us to spend time with them, but we need some time to ourselves, we may feel guilt or tension. By understanding how competing or conflicting needs and wants affect us we can find a balance to avoid unnecessary frustration or tension.

Balancing tension created by our needs and wants can be one of the most challeng-ing things we do. By having an awareness of our needs and wants, and how they motivate behavior, we can reduce our feelings of frustration and tension.

We were created by nature with needs and wants we cannot fulfill ourselves. Un-fulfilled needs and wants make us uncomfortable, and since we don't like being uncomfortable, we are motivated to take action to alleviate this discomfort by fulfilling them.

Since it is difficult for us to fulfill all our needs and wants on our own, we are motivated to get help from other people. In order to do this, we must be able to communicate with them. This is how our needs and wants motivate us to com-municate with one another.

The Nelsonian Laws of Communicating

As humans we were created by nature with needs and wants. Needs that must be fulfilled in order to survive and wants that motivate us to take action to fulfill them. We could have been created by nature to be simpler and less complicated with fewer needs and wants like other creatures on earth.

We could have been created with the ability to satisfy all our needs and wants by ourselves, but this was not how nature intended us to be. We were created with needs and wants, so we have to communicate with others in order to fulfill them. This means that the laws of communicating were created by nature because we were meant by nature to communicate and become involved with one another.

It is difficult to talk about communicating in and of itself because it is so closely linked with our behavior. Rarely do we communicate with someone and that's all. We communicate while we do things. We don't often do things without communicating about them and we don't often communicate without taking some kind of action.

Communicating and behavior are virtually inseparable because our behavior communicates information to others. How we communicate influences our behavior and the behavior of others. Our behavior has the ability to communicate information about us to others and other people's behavior communicates information about them. So, when this book refers to communicating what is actually being described is behavioral communicating.

Behavior is better understood when we know why people communicate because it gives what they do meaning. This process of behavioral communicating consists not only of how people use behavior to communicate, but how communicating affects behavior.

How we communicate with other people is shaped by the forces that motivate human behavior. These laws influence our behavior to comprise a *Grand Unified System of Human Behavior*. These laws have governed human behavior and how we communicate since the beginning of time. By understanding these laws and the forces they create, we can better understand human behavior and how we communicate.

The laws of behavioral communicating are analogous to the laws of nature or physics. They apply to everyone and do not change. These laws shape human behavior and how we communicate. They can be used to help understand what motivates human behavior including how and why we communicate with one another.

The author of this book is the first person to develop and apply new and innovative methodologies to understand how people are motivated by laws that govern communicating and behavior.

The author of this book is the first person to identify these laws, the *Nelsonian Laws of Uncertainty, Shared Meaning, and Investing*, which comprise a *Grand Unified Theory of Behavioral Communication*. These laws are in order of importance because the process begins with the first law and each preceding law is created by the ones before it.

Uncertainty

Life is uncertain. The world around us is chaotic. Things happen with no warning and for no apparent reason. We may know that things might happen, but do not know when or how. No one can predict the future or has the ability to control everything that might happen. Despite our best planning things do not go as we expect.

We experience things we do not want such as illness, financial troubles, and natural disasters. We are aware of our own mortality, even though we do not know when or how it will happen. All these things create uncertainty.

Uncertainty is the first and most important law of behavioral communicating because it makes the other two laws possible. It is like the law of gravity because it affects everyone and cannot be changed by people. No matter how much people seek to reduce uncertainty, it cannot be totally eliminated.

This is in part because we have needs and wants that must be fulfilled, because there are things about life we don't know, and because there are things that are out of our control.

Even if uncertainty could be totally eliminated, it would be detrimental for us and society. The law of uncertainty provides critical functions that shape who we are as individuals. Without uncertainty we would not be motivated to do the things that need to be done for society to function.

The degree of uncertainty we each experience is based on our individual perspectives and experiences. What constitutes uncertainty for one person may be viewed as a challenge or adventure for another.

Uncertainty is different for each person because it is based upon our past experiences, the degree to which our needs and wants are fulfilled, and the difference between our perceptions and expectations. Uncertainty can be viewed as the difference between how much security and stability we have in our life compared to what we need or want to have.

Uncertainty can affect our self-concept and how we interact with others based on the degree of confidence we have in ourselves and our abilities. It can be the difference between what we know and what we need or want to know. It can be the degree to which we feel we have some predictability about the future and having our expectations met.

Uncertainty occurs when reality, or our perception of reality, does not meet our expectations. Uncertainty can be measured by the degree to which there is a gap between our expectations and our perception of reality.

Uncertainty should not be considered the same as confusion or indecision. Confusion is a lack of clarity and indecision is the inability to make a decision. Uncertainty is not the same as doubt, which could be considered a lack of confidence in a person's competence or ability to affect a certain outcome.

Uncertainty is not the same as a risk. Uncertainty is created by nature whereas risk is generally created by people. Risk generally involves making choices about what is known, so we have an idea of what we stand to lose. Uncertainty is different because it represents the unknown, we don't know what we might gain or lose.

Uncertainty reduction.

Uncertainty can be uncomfortable, painful, even intolerable. It can create feelings of tension, frustration, and even anger. When we are faced with something that is uncomfortable we are motivated to reduce or eliminate it.

This is how the law of uncertainty motivates people to reduce uncertainty through the process of uncertainty reduction. We reduce uncertainty to reduce tension, frustration, and discomfort. Uncertainty reduction can help us to create predictability, stability, and security improving our quality of life. When bad things happen, we seek to understand them in order to reduce uncertainty and its impact on us.

It is our need for uncertainty reduction that has motivated most of human behavior throughout history. Much of what we have created in society has been done to improve our lives by reducing the effects that uncertainty has on us.

So, why don't we know everything we need to know? We may have been created by nature, but nature didn't reveal everything to us. We could have been created with all the knowledge we need about ourselves and the world around us from the time we are born.

Instead, we are forced to find things for ourselves leading to the creation of society as we know it today. Virtually everything that people have done since the beginning of time has been motivated by their need to reduce uncertainty in order to fulfill needs and wants.

By being unable to fulfill all our needs and wants, we are not always certain how they will be fulfilled. This creates uncertainty that can make us uncomfortable motivating us to take action. We want to know how our needs and wants will be fulfilled because we like stability and predictability, which it is comfortable.

In order to reduce uncertainty we have learned to communicate with one another, we have learned how to find out more about the world around us, and we have learned how to better understand ourselves.

From the moment we are born, as well as from the beginning of human history, we have been motivated by uncertainty to learn about themselves and the world around them, so that they could fulfill their needs and wants.

Without uncertainty we would not have the same motivation to communicate and work together with one another. This would make it less likely for people to have accomplished everything that has been accomplished throughout human history.

The origin of the law of uncertainty.

Since the earliest times in history, the law of uncertainty has motivated human behavior. We all have needs that must be fulfilled in order to survive, however, there is uncertainty about how they will be fulfilled. This led to the pursuit of uncertainty reduction, which has dominated most of human behavior throughout history.

At one time people were hunter gatherers roaming the countryside looking for game to hunt and food to harvest in order to fulfill their need to eat for survival. They fulfilled this need by hunting and gathering food, which led to a nomadic lifestyle moving to wherever food could be found. They didn't always know what they would find and if they did not find any food, they would go hungry. This way of life contained a high degree of uncertainty.

Motivated by the need to eat and the uncertainty of hunting and gathering, people developed alternatives like farming and ranching. By growing their own crops and raising livestock, people fulfilled their need to eat reducing uncertainty creating stability and predictability.

No longer needing to move from place to place, they could fulfill their needs by staying in one place for long periods of time. They could now invest their time and other resources in creating communities. So, uncertainty reduction to fulfill our basic needs led to the creation of many important institutions fundamental to developing society, making people's lives better by providing security and stability.

How uncertainty can be helpful.

Uncertainty can be helpful because it can open our mind to new ideas. It makes us question our assumptions and ascertain their validity. It motivates us to adapt and rethink what we already know. It motivates us to look at what we know in new ways to come up with something better than what we had before. It encourages us to change and try something new. And it motivates us to take action to do something about it.

However, we do not have to wait for difficulties caused by uncertainty to motivate us to look for new ideas and try new things. We can think about alternatives before we are forced to do so. While uncertainty may not always happen in positive ways, it does motivate us to look beyond what we already know.

So, why don't some things work out? When things work out for us the tension uncertainty creates is resolved. We feel more comfortable so there's less motivation to do something and we don't think as much about it. Our mind moves on to more pressing matters. If things don't work out, we need to think about them in order to work things through and look for alternative solutions.

When something doesn't work, it represents an unresolved state that creates tension making us uncomfortable motivating us to take action. It increases uncertainty motivating us to go beyond what we already know to gain new information and try new ways of doing things to resolve it.

We have lots of things we need to do, so we have to prioritize what to do first and the more something doesn't work out making us uncomfortable, the higher priority it gets. If everything worked out for us, we would be less likely to challenge ourselves, gain new knowledge, or open our mind to new possibilities.

Change is uncomfortable because it takes time and energy. So, in order for us to change, the current situation must become uncomfortable enough to overcome the discomfort it takes to change.

When we are aware of how this process works, we do not have to let uncertainty frustrate us, we can use it to our advantage. We can be open to new information and ideas to initiate change in our own time and on our own terms rather than being forced to change by circumstances. Uncertainty can be ironic, when we fail to take the initiative to do these things ourselves life can have a way of making us do it.

While reducing uncertainty can be a good thing, too much uncertainty reduction may not be good. When we are sure about what we are doing and feel like we have everything figured out, we are not looking for new information or new ideas.

In this frame of mind we can be less open to the possibilities that may be available to us. When we feel we have set goals, objectives, or a plan of action we may not consider that there may be better alternatives.

This state of mind can create reduced awareness of the situation, which limits our possibilities and options. When we think we know what to do, we have less motivation to look at other options. When we are less aware of what is around us we might pass up opportunities by pursuing a steadfast single path.

When we reduce uncertainty it increases our confidence motivating us to take action. The danger is that when people feel reduced uncertainty, they may not be open to new information, so it can close them off from considering other ideas or alternative ways of doing things.

This can cause them to filter out information and not listen to others who may have something to contribute. It can cause them to discount or filter out information that may be helpful. In extreme cases it can turn into arrogance creating an attitude that "I know what I'm doing." This can create the conditions that lead to bad decisions with potentially disastrous consequences.

This can happen when we are overly certain or when we think that we know what to do, so we do not stop and consider alternatives that might provide better choices. When we are certain, we are less likely to question our assumptions and the quality of our information. When we are certain, we do not look for flaws in our reasoning or test the validity of our solutions.

When we are certain, we are in the frame of mind to get things done the way that we want, rather than considering the ideas of others. When we are certain, we know that we are right and do not stop to think that we might be wrong. When we are certain, we do not need to learn anything because we know what we are doing. When we are certain, we do not look at different ideas and people who have them are viewed as disruptive troublemakers.

Extreme certainty should not be considered the same as knowledge, expertise, experience, or confidence. Knowledge gives us information we can use. Expertise can provide us information and skills to handle uncertainty. Experience hones those skills in actual situations. And confidence gives us a belief in ourselves and our abilities. We can have all these things while still utilizing uncertainty to bring in new ideas in order to innovate and facilitate change.

If everything was created for a reason, then uncertainty was created by nature for a reason, to provide us a means to motivate change and innovation. Having an awareness of how the law of uncertainty works helps us to avoid pitfalls, so we can use it to our advantage.

Uncertainty and the stop sign.

To illustrate how uncertainty affects our behavior think about what we do when we are driving and see a stop sign or stop light. We have to see the sign, understand what it means, and then act accordingly.

The sign does not stop our car, so why do we stop? We stop because of the law of uncertainty. Because there's a chance we might get hit by another vehicle or be pulled over and given a ticket that would cost us money. We stop because it reduces uncertainty giving us reasonable expectations of getting safely across the road.

Uncertainty can keep people within the limits of acceptable behavior. By not knowing the future results of our actions, we are more likely to be careful and less risky in our behavior because there is a fear of potential negative consequences.

The law of uncertainty motivates our behavior by keeping us within the rules of social reality and society. It inhibits us from taking too much risk or engaging in overly dangerous behavior. It motivates us to question ourselves and our actions, which is necessary in order to find the best solution and course of action.

All of our lives contain some degree of uncertainty. In order to reduce it, it is helpful to understand how it affects us in our own lives and in our business. What makes the difference is what we do about it. It is through increased awareness of how uncertainty works and how it acts in our lives that gives us options that will help us to reduce uncertainty and its effects.

Shared Meaning

The law of shared meaning is the second law of behavioral communicating. It is like the law of uncertainty in that it is created by nature, not by people. It is like the law of gravity because it affects everyone whether we want it to or not. It cannot be changed or eliminated. It affects how we communicate and share information with one another. It gives information significance to help make it useful to us.

This helps us make sense of our experiences. It helps us to understand ourselves and develop our self-concept. When something contains meaning it helps us access information from our experiences that may be useful, so we don't have to get all the information we need every time we communicate about something.

We are motivated by the law of uncertainty to create and share meaning, so that we can understand others to work with them and form relationships. This helps us to make sense out of our experiences to help explain what has happened in the past and better understand what we can expect in the future. Sharing meaning helps develop feelings of security and stability because we have a better understanding of others and the world around us.

Our life consists of a series of experiences, some of which may not make sense motivating us to wonder why they happen and what we can do about them. In order to reduce the uncertainty that would be created if these were just random events, we want to understand them better by looking for meaning in them.

In order to do this, we share our experiences with others and they share their experiences with us. Sharing our experiences with others creates mutual understanding, which gives us a deeper meaning reducing uncertainty to make things more understandable in the future.

Much of how our identity is created is through our experiences and sharing meaning about them. How we communicate about our experiences helps develop our self-concept and identity. When we share our experiences with others they learn who we are and we learn about them. We all have needs and wants, and others must help us to fulfill them. The law of shared meaning helps us to do this.

Throughout history people have wanted to know more about what was happening in the world around them. This motivated them to understand things like the changing of the seasons, how to grow crops, why they got sick, and their relationship with God. As people encountered uncertainty they looked for ways to understand what they experienced.

Early Greek and Roman cultures sought to explain what they experienced by creating mythology. Later, people looked to religions and sacred texts. More recently people utilized science and empirical research methods to understand the world around them. These approaches helped them to create and share meaning to better understand themselves, others, and the world around them.

The law of shared meaning affects how we interpret our observations, thoughts, feelings, and experiences to make sense of them. It shapes our view of practically everything. In order to reduce uncertainty, we need to know more about others, ourselves, and the things around us.

We can get information for ourselves, but that takes time and energy. So, we get it from others. In order to do this, people developed language to share information utilizing symbols, which are invested with meaning. We also use nonverbal information by investing practically everything around us with meaning. To reduce uncertainty we need a means to share information by communicating. This is how the law of uncertainty creates the law of shared meaning.

How the law of shared meaning works.

You have likely experienced how the law of shared meaning works. Have you ever attended a party, wedding, or other event with a friend who knew everyone, but you didn't know anyone? They probably talked, laughed, and shared stories about mutual friends with one another. If you didn't know anyone there you probably felt awkward, out of place, maybe even wanted to leave.

This is how the law of shared meaning works. The others were able to find meaning in who they saw and what they said. This made the experience more meaningful to them, while you probably didn't know what they were talking about. What you experienced is what things could be like if there was no shared meaning.

The law of shared meaning can be illustrated by how we interpret information. To show how this works, find a book that has pictures of people you know and another book that has pictures of people you don't know, along with their names and some kind of other information about them like a school yearbook. Look at pictures of people you don't know. You can see what they look like, read their names, and understand the information about them.

You probably won't have much additional information about who they are other than what is printed. Now look at the book with pictures of people you know. Read their names and the information about them. You might recall things about them, things they did, perhaps even feelings or emotions. What you are thinking and feeling contains information that is beyond what is printed in the book.

When we see people we know, we recall things about them like the things that they did, perhaps even feelings or emotions. You might have feelings of warmth and affection or perhaps dislike or agitation. You might remember things that you did together that makes you laugh. What you are thinking and feeling contains information that is beyond what is happening in the present. It's like a connection is made and something opens up. It's a very different experience than when we see or talk to people we don't know.

If there were no law of shared meaning, what we communicate to others would be more like looking at pictures of people we don't know. We could communicate with one another, but there would be little additional information available making it more difficult to understand them. We would have to explain practically everything every time we communicated.

Having shared meaning gives us a reserve of information that we can call up without having to communicate it or have it explained to us every time we needed it. Shared meaning is how we make sense of the world around us. It is how we interpret our observations, thoughts, feelings, and experiences. It shapes our view of practically everything because it influences how we see ourselves, others, and the world around us.

The origin of the law of shared meaning.

Since our needs and wants motivate us to take action by communicating with others, sharing meaning helps us determine what actions to take. The meanings we share can determine our behavior. For example, we share meaning about things like the weather.

At one time, people found meaning in the lack of rain and the failure of their crops to grow as God's displeasure with them. They might even have made sacrifices to their gods. Today, when there's a lack of rain we interpret it as weather patterns brought by the jet stream and build irrigation systems. This means that the same set of circumstances, influenced by different shared meanings, motivates distinctly different behavior.

When we communicate with others we look for shared meaning not only in what they say, but also in what they do. We find meaning in what people do, how they look, their facial expressions, and other nonverbal elements. Meaning is found not just in the words people say, but also in how they say them. We look for meaning in these things so we can understand others better to reduce our uncertainty about them.

The nature of shared meaning.

Shared meaning gives us a sense of our identity as an individual and as a member of groups. Through the process of shared meaning when we communicate with others they respond with feedback that affects our perception of who we are. We share different meanings with others based upon the nature of our relationship with them such as our friends, family, or coworkers.

We get a broader perspective about our experiences when we share them with others. When many people share their experiences, it creates a common history that develops culture. It is through shared meaning that we come to understand our relationships with other people.

We share meaning about what other people say and do in order to reduce uncertainty and to make them more familiar. When people are unfamiliar, we do not know what they might do and so we can be less willing to communicate or work with them. However, we need others to help us fulfill our needs and wants which motivates us to find meaning in what they do.

So, we gather information by observing what people say and do. In order for that information to be useful, we interpret it by giving it meaning. We often don't have enough information so we make inferences to fill in what's missing. This gives us an idea of what a person is like so that we know what we can reasonably expect from them to reduce uncertainty.

The law of shared meaning enables us to share knowledge so that we can learn from the experiences of others. Many of the things we want to know have already been done by someone else, so we can benefit from their knowledge and experience through the process of shared meaning. We can make their experiences useful for us without needing to have the same experiences. Without the law of shared meaning, developing and sharing knowledge would be more difficult.

The law of shared meaning makes it possible to communicate with each other using a common language. Language is the means by which people create symbols, like letters and words, and invest them with meaning. Sharing meaning enables us to communicate with one another using a language that everyone understands.

We invest meaning in people like our family, friends, coworkers, or neighbors. We give meaning to our past experiences in order to add significance to our lives. We give meaning to the things that we enjoy such as art, literature, and music.

We give meaning to geographic locations like where we were born or where we live. We give meaning to our culture, ethnicity, nationality, and religion. Practically everything we do, everyone we know, and everything around us we invest with meaning and we share these meanings by communicating with others.

Traditions and rituals like holidays, celebrations, birthdays, anniversaries, and other occasions when people get together are an important way that we share meaning. We celebrate these events because of their significance and participate in them to share their meaning through our actions.

Sharing traditions and rituals gives us a sense of who we are, where we have come from in the past, and our expectations for the future. It makes us feel closer to others and part of a group with whom we share the same experiences. It reduces uncertainty giving us a feeling of stability and security.

By sharing meanings we communicate what our country stands for and what it means to be a citizen. We communicate our history and traditions, values and beliefs. These shared meanings can be understood by members of a society as well as outsiders. How people share meaning can be a powerful force because it has the ability to motivate their attitudes and actions on a large scale.

The law of shared meaning leads to investing because when people give things meaning they also give them value. Giving something meaning gives it significance and significance increases its importance making it more valuable. This is because when something is important to us we are willing to do more or spend more to obtain it or keep it.

We place value on people and relationships, on things and possessions, on intangible concepts such as skills or knowledge, and on practically everything we find around us. Value is often based on comparisons gained from our perceptions to create expectations. We use our perception based on currently available information and compare it to our expectations for the future. This can motivate us to rank things by their importance, which can help us to set priorities.

We often value things based on how useful they are to us in fulfilling our needs and wants. Shared meaning can determine what objects we value. We place value on things that we feel an emotional attachment to or that are part of our past experiences. Sometimes how much we value something comes from what others think about it.

Through the process of shared meaning, if enough people value something others are more likely to place a value on it. By sharing meaning we come to know how important, valuable, and useful things are. In this way sharing meaning has tangible and monetary consequences.

Investing

The law of investing is the third law of behavioral communicating. It is similar to the laws of uncertainty and shared meaning because it was created by nature, so it cannot be changed by people. It is like the law of gravity because it affects everyone whether we want it to or not.

The law of investing was formed by the other two laws in order to make them work. We can reduce uncertainty and share meaning, but we need to take action for anything to happen. In order to reduce uncertainty and share meanings, we must invest our time and other resources in ourselves and others.

People may react to the first two laws by simply hunkering down and building a cabin in the woods. However, the law of investing forces them out into the marketplace of human activity.

The law of investing regulates how we manage our resources and negotiate with others for our mutual benefit to fulfill needs and wants, so we can accomplish our desired outcomes.

This creates a kind of behavioral communicative marketplace where people make and receive offers utilizing their resources to obtain their desired outcomes. Communicating is the currency of this marketplace because it enables us to invest these resources. This is the fundamental process that makes human behavior work by connecting us to others.

We all have needs and wants that we cannot fulfill ourselves, so we need help from others to fulfill them. Other people also have their own needs and wants that they cannot fulfill themselves, so they also need help. This puts everyone in the position of wanting things, but needing help from others to obtain them.

We have resources of value that others need and they have resources we want. The most familiar resource is monetary, but we more often utilize other resources like our time, attention, effort, energy, expertise, experience, and skills. When we have unfulfilled needs and wants it can be uncomfortable motivating us to communicate with others, so we can invest in relationships to achieve our mutual desired outcomes.

When this process goes smoothly everyone benefits, however, it often does not. People can have virtually unlimited needs and wants to fulfill with limited resources. We often have conflicting needs and wants. We may feel we are contributing to others, but not receiving what we need in return.

This can create tension or conflict, which can force us to make choices about our relationships and how we communicate with others. For example, if we are in a relationship where the other person is only taking and our needs are not being met, we might want to end it. This is how the law of investing can exert powerful forces that motivate our behavior, the decisions we make, and how we communicate with others.

In order to invest in others we need to reduce uncertainty. When we feel a great deal of uncertainty, we can be more reluctant to invest our resources because we do not know what to expect.

When we reduce uncertainty, we are more likely to invest because we feel more safe and secure because we have reasonable expectations about the future. The less uncertainty we feel the more comfortable we are sharing our resources in order to help others fulfill their needs and wants. This also makes it more likely for them to help us fulfill ours.

Not only do we seek to reduce uncertainty so we can invest, but we also invest to reduce uncertainty. We invest our resources in relationships and activities that will benefit us now and in the future. For example, we invest time and energy in a job to receive not only a salary, but also for the safety and security that comes with it. This can help us to fulfill other needs such as buying a house, having a family, or retirement.

The law of shared meaning helps us to invest because it increases our mutual understanding of one another. When we share meaning with others, we feel we get to know them better so we know what to expect of them in the future. This can increase stability and security making us feel more comfortable investing our resources.

The more we feel safe and secure, the more we are likely to invest ourselves and our resources in relationships without expecting an immediate return. This helps create the long term stability necessary for creating and maintaining meaningful relationships.

The marketplace of communicating.

When we communicate with others we make offers that are either accepted or rejected. This process works rather like the trading floor of a stock market. This happens in our daily activities like when we ask people for help, initiate relationships, negotiate family responsibilities, and get things done at work. This happens as we go about our daily activities, so it goes mostly unnoticed.

This marketplace is driven by how we communicate with each other so communicating could be characterized as its currency. In order to fulfill needs and wants, people enter the marketplace and negotiate with others by offering resources and seeking investments in return. It is through communicating that we negotiate what we are willing to do and what we might expect in return.

We can have a balance sheet in the back of our mind where we keep track of the return on our investments. If they are reasonably balanced we feel satisfied, however, if they are out of balance and we feel we are contributing more than we receive it can create unhappiness, tension, even conflict.

We want to know how our investments are doing and so we make comparisons with other people we think are similar to see how they are doing. For example, if we feel we should be making more money, we might look around to see how much other people are making or if we can get a better job. If we feel that we are doing well, we feel good about ourselves. If we are not, then we may look to change things.

We look at needs and wants fulfillment in both the long and short term much like we look at monetary investments. The longer the investment the higher the expectation for greater benefits.

For example, people make financial sacrifices with the expectation of future financial security including savings, home ownership, or self-fulfillment. We are willing to wait longer for these benefits because they fulfill more important needs and wants.

Communicating can be an indicator of value in a business. People tend to communicate about things that are important to them, so you can determine what they value by measuring the amount of time and effort they spend communicating about something.

We do not communicate about things that are not important or we are not interested in. To effectively communicate with others, it's helpful to know what they value. This can be measured by the amount of time they spend communicating about it.

By listening to others, we can know what is of value to them and determine what would make them more likely to invest. So, it's possible to analyze what is going on in any communicating marketplace by measuring its activity. This works rather like stock prices or economic indicators.

Observing how people communicate and what they communicate about can be used to evaluate the health and effectiveness of an organization including member satisfaction and commitment.

Conventional wisdom would suggest that in a marketplace people would seek to minimize costs and maximize rewards, in other words they buy low and sell high. However, when it comes to communicating with others, this may be more the exception than the rule.

This is because when one person seems to be benefiting more than others, it creates an imbalance, others may feel that they are not being treated fairly. People do not like to be around someone who contributes as little as possible while seeking to gain as much as possible by buying low and selling high.

Not everyone looks to maximize rewards, instead they look to fulfill their needs and wants. They may be satisfied by being slightly ahead, breaking even, or even having a small loss.

This makes the break even point or achieving economic equilibrium an important factor in determining work satisfaction, so everyone receives fair rewards and feels like they are being treated fairly.

Some people behave contrary to conventional wisdom by forgoing their own safety and material comfort to live in arduous conditions to help others. They may give up lucrative careers to pursue endeavors that pay very little.

While this behavior does not follow the convention of buy low sell high, it follows the laws of uncertainty and investing because people invest in order to fulfill their individual needs and wants, which can reduce their feelings of uncertainty.

Motivated by the law of investing, they are maximizing their investment based on their perception of what fulfills their needs and wants. This is because our needs and wants are more than just monetary, they can be spiritual, being needed by others, making a difference, feeling appreciated, or doing the right thing.

When people want monetary benefits, what they may really need is to feel appreciated. For most people the benefits that are the most important to them are generally not material or monetary.

The law of investing can affect how happy we feel. All too often we find ourselves in situations that aren't working and then wonder what's wrong. How we balance costs and rewards can be an indicator of several things.

In order to better understand what these things are, you can create a balance sheet by listing your needs and wants in order of importance. For each one, ask yourself how well are each of them being met?

When they are being reasonably met, it can make us feel good. When they are not being met, we can feel unhappy, even frustrated. When we understand how the law of investing works, we are more likely to be satisfied and feel good about ourselves when we feel we are making fair investments and receiving fair rewards.

Chapter 3
How Communicating Works

The Rules of Communicating

The laws of uncertainty, shared meaning, and investing were created by nature to motivate human behavior. In order for people to effectively utilize these laws, they developed the rules of communicating.

Rules govern our behavior by letting us know what is expected of us in just about every aspect of life. Businesses could not run without them. Rules tell people how to reduce uncertainty, they regulate how people share meaning, and they let people know what they can expect when investing in themselves and others.

Rules help us to fulfill our needs and wants, so we agree to abide by them because if we did not, life would be chaotic and it would be almost impossible to function. Rules allow the marketplace of communicating to function properly, so people can create relationships in order to fulfill their needs and wants.

Nearly all human activities, groups, and organizations have their own set of rules, which have been developed to meet people's needs and wants by regulating their behavior. Rules are necessary in order to reduce uncertainty so that people know what is expected of them and what they can expect from others.

A good example of why rules were created and how they work is illustrated by those used in sports. Many of the sports that we are familiar with today, like basketball or football, at one time did not exist. They were created by people who got together to fulfill mutual needs and wants like having fun, to compete, or to be part of a team.

In order for them to do this they had to create rules to govern their behavior, so that everyone knew what to expect. The rules changed over time to meet their changing needs. Without rules no one would know what to do and everything would breakdown into chaos.

Rules are created by people so they can work together to fulfill their needs and wants. For rules to work everyone must agree to abide by them so they know what to expect. Rules facilitate the process of shared meaning to reduce uncertainty and encourage investing in others. They enable us to communicate more effectively with one another, which helps us to achieve our desired outcomes.

The Process of Communicating

The process of communicating provides a way to look at how we communicate by understanding individual elements in the process. It helps us to see how these elements work together so that we can be better understood by other people. We often communicate without thinking how things work, so when they don't go as we want, like when we are misunderstood, we may not know how to fix them.

By understanding the process of communicating, you can develop skills to communicate more effectively with other people. How people communicate involves a number of elements that occur seamlessly so that we don't think much about them.

It can be helpful to break the process down into its elements to show how it works. You, your desired outcome, your Great Idea, others, connections, The Great Abyss, feedback, and effectiveness are all elements in the process of communicating.

Being aware of these elements and how they work provides a way to talk about how we communicate, so that we can communicate more effectively with others.

You.

You are the creator of your message, so the process of communicating begins with you. Everyone has their own style of communicating. Some characteristics that influence your style include your background, interests, and experiences.

Everyone has a different set of communicating skills. This can affect how they communicate with others because people who have well developed skills tend to feel more confident, so they can be more likely to communicate with others especially in uncertain situations.

People who feel they do not have communicating skills tend to hold back and may not participate as fully. This can give a false impression that they are not interested or are aloof. So, it can be helpful to develop communicating skills.

Desired outcome.

We communicate not only to share information and to understand each other, but also to get things done. We often determine what we want in terms of achieving goals and objectives, but desired outcome is different.

Goals and objectives can be specific things we want to achieve, so we develop a plan and pursue a course of action that can put us on a single path leaving little room for other ways to achieve them.

This approach can prevent us from noticing alternatives that may be preferable. There may even be a chance that the goal we are pursuing is not the best one for us.

We often characterize getting what we want as achieving a goal or objective. Using sports as an example, a goal or objective can be considered analogous to making a goal, basket, home run, or touchdown. It is a clear, definite action that is either accomplished or not. Since not every team can win every game, goals and objectives can be discouraging. They can even hurt your self-concept and sense of well being.

A desired outcome approach would focus more on a general sense of well being like personal growth and development, working better as a team, and enjoyment of the game. While losing a game will not accomplish your objective, you can still achieve your desired outcome.

Desired outcome is what you want to happen after others get your message. It is more general in nature and considers the big picture, which gives you more ways to achieve what you want. Desired outcome encourages you to consider more than one path to select the most effective one and to change them as needed.

This lets you to pursue opportunities you might find along the way. Desired outcome focuses less on achieving specific goals or objectives and more on fulfilling needs and wants, which provides more flexibility in how you fulfill them.

Desired outcome is about what you want to happen after you communicate with others, rather than looking for something specific to happen, take a big picture approach focusing on your general state of well being. This increases the number of ways to reach your desired outcome providing you with more flexibility.

Increased flexibility can improve your effectiveness and the likelihood that you make it happen. It can reduce the pressure to win by reducing the prospect of not achieving your goal. If one approach doesn't work, there may be other ways to achieve your desired outcome. This helps to create a more positive climate that can encourage others to work with you.

When you know your desired outcome you can spend time on what really matters. Everyone has tasks to accomplish, but desired outcomes are more than that. Simply accomplishing tasks themselves may not achieve our desired outcomes.

This can be why we might feel that we are working all the time, but not getting anywhere. This could be one reason successful people may be frustrated, because they focus on accomplishing tasks or achieving goals and objectives, while neglecting their desired outcomes.

Focusing on achieving your desired outcome can be a more positive approach because it is less discouraging when what you want to happen does not happen. It helps us avoid thinking about things as being good and bad or feeling like a failure. It allows us to find partial success in what we do because pursuing a desired outcome considers your general state of well being.

Businesses tend to focus on achieving goals and objectives. We often have a list of tasks we are expected to do. However, doing these tasks may not achieve your true desired outcome by getting the results you want. Goals and objectives tend to focus on you, or the person who does them.

A desired outcome approach looks at the person you communicate with to approach things from their perspective. Once you have determined your desired outcome, you can then set goals and objectives to achieve that and it's easier to change things if needed.

There are times when we try to achieve our desired outcome and things don't go the way we would like them to go. These situations could be characterized as resulting in unintended or undesired outcomes.

An unintended outcome is a result that we did not expect, it can be positive or negative or a little bit of both. An undesired outcome is when we get a result we do not want. Because it is undesired, it is generally considered negative.

No matter how effectively we communicate there is always the possibility that instead of achieving our desired outcome, we might get an undesired or unintended outcome.

Your Great Idea.

Your Great Idea is the message you want to communicate. It is the information you communicate to others. It begins with your message, which is what you say or write, but it can also consist of many other elements such as nonverbal information including facial expressions and gestures. It starts with an idea that exists in your mind not just in words, but also in pictures.

In order to communicate Your Great Idea to others, it has to be in a form that they can understand. This usually involves putting ideas into words that are spoken or written.

The words and letters themselves are just symbols that have no inherent meaning. The meaning is given to the symbols by people who translate them into words in order to communicate them to others.

When they receive the message, they translate the words back into ideas to understand them. We use the law of shared meaning to go through this process of investing symbols with meaning and translating that meaning into ideas. We do this so often it happens naturally without much thought.

When we speak, our mind automatically translates our ideas into words and when we read or hear words they are converted into ideas. This means that the meanings are in the minds of people and not necessarily in the symbols themselves.

For example, when you see the word TREE, you don't think oh, that's four letters. In your mind you see a picture of a big green plant with a trunk, branches, and leaves or needles. This is because everyone who understands English has learned that these four letters are symbols that represent a big green thing.

The word TREE is not actually a living tree. Using symbols is critical to communicating because if every time we wanted to communicate the idea of a tree, we would have to describe it or show one to others and that would take a lot of time.

Instead, we take the symbols T R E E and invest them with meaning so the letters become a shorthand reference that refers to the real big green thing.

Others.

Others are the people with whom you communicate. In the process of communicating, everything begins with you so anyone else you communicate with whether it's just one person or a large number of people are referred to as "others." Just as you communicate with others for a reason, others listen and communicate with you for reasons of their own.

Since every person is unique, other people have their own way of doing things, which includes their own style of communicating. This includes their individual characteristics that give them their own personality. These characteristics can affect how they communicate with you.

To communicate effectively, it is helpful to know and recognize the unique communicating styles of others to help adapt your own communicating style to them, while still being you.

The same things that influence your style of communicating such as family, culture, education, religion, and geographic affiliation also influence how others communicate with you.

How others communicate is based upon their background and experiences. No two people have the same experiences, even those who grew up in the same family. Even people who experience the same events have different perceptions of them.

Others are more likely to communicate about things that they are interested in or that they like. In order to effectively communicate with others, it's helpful to be aware of what things might influence how and why others communicate with you.

No matter how much you may want to, you cannot change how other people communicate and what they do. However, you can change the way that you communicate with them. By having an awareness of the process of communicating and how it affects others, you can adapt your own style to communicate more effectively with them.

Connections.

Once you have created your Great Idea you need a connection to get it to others. A connection is the means by which you reach to others so that they can hear or see your message.

Creating a connection is essential to effectively communicating with others. If there is no connection, they cannot get your message. Some common connections include speaking face to face, telephone calls, writing a letter or email, public speaking, or through the media.

We make connections with others through our five senses. When we speak or listen to someone, we make an auditory connection. We use gestures and facial expressions such as smiling to communicate nonverbally, so others see us through a visual connection.

Shaking hands or patting someone on the back makes a connection using touch. Wearing perfume or cologne or offering them food makes a connection using our sense of smell. Sharing food or drink, like dinner or coffee makes a connection utilizing taste. Most of the time making a connection involves using more than one of our five senses.

We all have different ways that we obtain and retain information. So, when you use multiple connections appealing to more than one sense, you increase the chance that people understand and remember your message. For example, if you want your children to be on time for dinner, you could utilize multiple connections through different senses.

You can use an auditory connection by telling them. You can use a visual connection by leaving a note on the refrigerator where they will see it. You can use smell to make a connection by having food that smells good to attract their attention. Increasing the number of connections can make an experience more intense.

The Great Abyss.

In the process of communicating, you communicate your Great Idea to others by making connections with them in order to achieve your desired outcome. In an ideal situation they would receive and understand your message, however, in reality other things can get in the way. Making a connection with others does not necessarily mean that they will understand your message.

Sometimes when you communicate with others, there is a huge chasm that separates you from them. In order to effectively communicate with others, you must make a connection to get your message across this chasm without it getting lost. This chasm can be characterized as "The Great Abyss."

The Great Abyss can alter how people perceive your message and even stop it from getting through to them. It can be thought of like a swamp or chasm that has to be crossed to make a connection with them. It represents what can get in the way of you communicating with others, so that they don't get your message.

Instead, they may get a different idea, the wrong message, or nothing at all which could result in undesired or unintended outcomes. This is why understanding what is in The Great Abyss can be helpful to effectively communicate with others.

The Great Abyss consists of interference that prevents others from understanding your Great Idea. You can interfere with your own message when it is unclear, confused, or disorganized. This can be overcome by using methods of organization, clarifying information, and seeking feedback from others to make sure they clearly understand your Great Idea.

Interference can come from others because they have their own ideas that may interfere with what you want to communicate to them. You can cut through it by emphasizing key points, repeating important information, seeking out feedback or asking questions. By cutting through the interference you can help others better understand your message.

External interference comes from things that people hear in their physical surroundings. This interference can mask or distract others from hearing and fully understanding your message. Internal interference comes from things that occur in people's minds that interferes with how they perceive your Great Idea. They may have a short attention span, their mind wanders, or they think about other things.

Point of view is how people see things including themselves, others, and the world around them. Everyone has their own point of view which is based on their past experiences. It affects how they interpret and understand your message. By being aware of their point of view, you can communicate more effectively with them.

A frame of reference is like the frame of a window or the viewfinder of a camera. It frames what a person sees or wants to see and everything outside the frame is blocked out or ignored. People can choose what things to let through their frames and what things to keep out.

People tend to block out information that is contrary to what they feel they already know. We are inundated with so many messages we filter out many of them and pay attention to only a small amount of information that is communicated to us. However, if we need or want something we are less likely to filter it out.

By being aware of potential sources of interference, you can communicate in ways that minimize their impact by eliminating as many of them as possible. Using repetition, emphasizing important points, and soliciting feedback can help to cut through this type of interference.

Feedback.

So, you have your Great Idea, made a connection, and crossed The Great Abyss to communicate it to others. How do you know if they got your message? Utilizing feedback is the best way to find out how well your Great Idea has been received.

Feedback can happen in a variety of ways. It can happen informally by asking questions or having others restate your ideas to determine if they fully understand them. Feedback can happen in formal ways such as surveys, interviews, polls, or focus groups that can be used to determine the effectiveness of your message.

It is important that feedback be accurate and honest. A face to face conversation is the best means of feedback because it is instantaneous and offers the widest variety of channels to communicate.

Other types of feedback such as customer comment cards, surveys, and polls can be helpful, but may be less accurate as people may not be motivated to participate, may provide incomplete information, or give the answers they think makes them look the best.

Effectiveness.

Effectiveness is the degree to which others understand your Great Idea and you achieve your desired outcome. We might characterize some ways of communicating as good and some as bad.

For example, if someone doesn't understand us, we might think that we did a bad job of communicating with them. If we speak in front of a group and it doesn't go well, we may feel that we are not a good speaker.

Thinking about communicating in these terms does not let us to look at what happened in a way that helps us to improve our skills, which can be discouraging. If we feel things didn't go so well, it can increase our anxiety making us reluctant to do it again. A speech that might have been considered bad could in fact have been somewhat effective in getting your message across. Then you can look at how to make it more effective.

Rather than thinking in terms of good or bad, think of communicating effectively. Effective communicating is the degree to which you achieve your desired outcome. The more you understand others and the more they understand you, the more effectively you can communicate with them.

Looking at how you communicate in terms of effectiveness rather than good or bad can help you to determine what works and what could be improved. It can give you a more realistic idea of your skills, so that you can feel better about what you can do and work on developing what could be done better.

Styles of Communicating

When people create their Great Idea they may use a particular style of communicating. How they communicate can be characterized by three basic styles.

The first style, the arrow approach.

This style of communicating is like shooting an arrow into the air and hoping it hits the target. In this approach, a person creates their Great Idea, they construct a message, send it to others through a connection, and then wait for the result. The people who receive it may not fully understand the message or may interpret it differently than it was intended.

While this sounds like an ineffective way to communicate that can create misunderstandings, it is how people have been communicating for a long time. Much of the news and information we receive that affects our perceptions and expectations is communicated through the media using this approach.

This method of communicating is based on a military model where a commanding officer sends a message down the chain of command to the troops in the field who are expected to follow orders. Then the commander waits for the result. This style was considered successful so it was adopted by businesses, but it lacks an effective means to provide feedback to know if a message was received or understood.

The second style, the tennis approach.

This style of communicating resolves some of the problems with the first style. It encourages the person receiving the message to communicate back to the person who sent it to determine how well it was understood. The original sender could then decide if additional information is necessary to clarify it.

This approach works like tennis where one person creates their Great Idea and then hits it over the net hoping the other person will get it. If the other person returns the ball your message has been received.

We use this style when we send emails, memos, and phone messages. This style offers some improvement over the first method because there is a way to provide feedback to clarify the original message. It is commonly used even though it can be awkward and time consuming.

The third style, the conversational approach.

This style of communicating fixes most of the problems of the first and second styles. It is more realistic and effective because it takes into account all aspects of the process of communicating.

It works like having a conversation where the people involved are talking to one another. They are communicating information and providing feedback simultaneously. It is the most effective approach, however, it can take the most energy. It is often preferred because it takes into account the people involved and the situation.

This style is called a conversational style because it is like having a conversation where people both speak and listen as well as provide information and ask questions simultaneously.

This style works well in situations where instantaneous feedback helps the process. For example, if you are trying to fix a computer it can be difficult reading a manual and could take forever using email. Having a conversation provides direct feedback to make the process easier.

We use this style when we see someone face to face and have a conversation or when we speak to them over the telephone. This style is a more effective means of communicating because we get results immediately rather than waiting for feedback, saving time.

For example, a short conversation can accomplish more than many emails because we can communicate exactly what we want, clarify information, answer questions, and resolve things much more quickly.

However, people may avoid doing this by using the other two styles like texting and emailing because they can be reviewed and edited before sending. They may feel conversation is too spontaneous or risky increasing anxiety and uncertainty.

In order to communicate more effectively, it is helpful to recognize when to use each of these styles of communicating and why. While the third style is the most effective, consider just how often people use the first two.

We tend to get in the habit of using the first two styles because they can be easier and quicker. They save us time and allow us to make a connection, while still keeping a distance. Each of these styles can be useful depending on your desired outcome, but they also have their limitations.

Chapter 4
Creating a Great You

What if you were on stage in a play, but didn't know your lines or even what play you were in? What would you do?

What if you were in front of an audience to give a speech, but didn't know what to say or why you were there? What would you do?

While this would probably never happen, these situations are similar to how we learn to communicate. From the time we are born, we encounter unfamiliar situations when we may not know what we should say or do. So, we learn as we go by communicating with others.

Communicating can be considered similar to acting or musical performance. Your audience needs to clearly understand you, which requires a certain amount of skill. Since communicating is something we do every day, we may give little consideration to developing these skills.

However, like acting or music, in order to effectively communicate with others it is helpful to develop communicating skills and abilities. Effectively communicating with others begins by having an awareness of how we communicate with ourselves.

Many professionals like musicians and actors study fundamentals and basic techniques of their craft in order to develop the skills essential for a successful performance. A similar approach can be taken to communicating. There are fundamental skills that can be developed to help you effectively communicate with others.

So, how do you know what you know?

In the past people developed knowledge that they believed to be true, which we now know is not. Consider that a second century astronomer determined that the sun and all the planets revolved around the earth. In medieval times, it was thought that alchemy could turn lead into gold.

In colonial times, some women were thought to be witches. More recently, it was thought that cigarettes had health benefits because they were both a stimulant and relaxant.

So, how do you know what is right? How do we know what we consider to be true today might be proven to be not true in the future?

Since people utilize the law of shared meaning to create knowledge as a part of their social reality, this raises an important question. If enough people decide that something is right, does that make it right?

Some societies thought that human sacrifices or the burning of witches was right. So, what are we doing today that we consider right because some people perceive it's right, but may not be in the future?

Throughout history people of different cultures from different geographic regions had similar experiences, faced similar problems, and accomplished similar tasks.

They often had the same needs and wants that they sought to fulfill. Even though they have many similarities, they developed different solutions based upon their view of social reality.

So, how do we come to know what we know? We all have our own way of obtaining information to know what we know. Much of what we know we learn through education and experience. This can make it difficult to change what people think they know. They may resist new information, perhaps becoming defensive.

Rather than trying to convince them to change, challenge them to think beyond what they know to gain new knowledge. This can get people to think beyond what they see as true. People may resist changing what they believe, but they are less likely to want to be perceived as being unwilling to learn something new.

When we want to know something, how do we learn about it? We create knowledge in the following ways to help us understand the world around us.

Perceiving. Gaining knowledge through our five senses; sight, sound, touch, taste, smell.

Doing. Gaining knowledge through experience by participating.

Thinking. Gaining knowledge through education, rationality, logic, or scientific inquiry.

Believing. Gaining knowledge through religion or faith by trusting in something unseen.

Realizing. Gaining knowledge through instinct or revelation.

Feeling. Gaining knowledge through intuition, emotions, or empathy.

Knowledge is not just about how we gain information, it's also about how we use it. Gaining new knowledge works like the perception process where we select, organize, and interpret information to give it meaning so it fits in with what we already know. How this happens is influenced by the law of uncertainty. When we feel uncertainty, we are more likely to be open to new knowledge.

When uncertainty is reduced, people can feel more self-assured about themselves and what they are doing, so they may not be open to new ideas or different ways of thinking. When someone is overly certain, they are not necessarily open to other ideas. Throughout history, many people were certain about things they believed to be true, which has sometimes resulted in disastrous consequences.

Perception

Perception is how we gather information and give it meaning, so that it can be useful to us. We gather information through our five senses: sight, sound, taste, touch, and smell. We also gather information through other means such as our feelings, emotions, intuition, and impressions.

Perception is more than just receiving information, it is about what we do with this information. It is how we make sense of ourselves, others, and the world around us. Perception gives meaning to our experiences. It provides us with the information we use to solve problems and make decisions. It is how we develop our attitudes, formulate our beliefs, and establish our values.

By understanding how the perception process works, we can become more aware of our choices and have more control over how we use the information we receive. We perceive information all the time without thinking much about it, however, effectively utilizing it takes effort. Having an awareness of how the perception process works enables us to take control of the information we perceive rather than letting it control our thoughts and actions.

The perception process is motivated by the law of uncertainty. It is through our perceptions that we gain information and knowledge to reduce uncertainty about ourselves, others, and the world around us.

The perception process is how we share meaning with others. It's how we gather, organize, and give information meaning so that it is useful to us now and in the future. The perception process provides the basis for how we make decisions and solve problems. It makes the process of communicating work.

Interference can hinder our perceptions blocking out potentially important information. Our filters and frames of reference determine what information we actually perceive. By being aware of the perception process and how it works, we can improve our own communicating skills to communicate more effectively with others to reduce uncertainty.

Perception includes listening, speaking, tasting, touching, and smelling as well as intuition and feelings. The perception process includes selection, organization, and interpretation of what we perceive, so that it can be useful to us now and in the future.

Selection.

Selection involves what information we choose to perceive, what is important to us, and what is not. There is often more information available to us than we can use, so we must decide what to keep and what to discard. It's a natural process so we generally don't think much about it.

We are more likely to pay attention to things we like or that we find interesting. We often select information that fits in with what we already know because it fulfills our expectations reducing uncertainty. We tend to filter out information that is unfamiliar or contradicts what we already know because it can be uncomfortable.

Organization.

Organization is how we arrange, sort, categorize, and fit together the information we perceive. Information doesn't always come to us in a clearly organized way, so we need to arrange it in a way that's meaningful to us. How information is organized directly affects its meaning and how we utilize it. We do this because when information is organized it reduces uncertainty and we can give it meaning. This makes it easier to recall making it useful to us in the future.

However, this process doesn't always go easily and we may be missing pieces, so we have to fill in the missing information to make sense. We fill in the gaps by using inferences and other information that may not be true or accurate.

When we come across something new we tend to organize it based upon our existing categories. If something doesn't fit into our categories, we are more likely to discard it. This is because grouping information together makes it easier for us to organize and recall it later.

The perception process works a bit like books in a library. The books are organized by topics making it easy for us to find and use them. There is an established method to how they are organized so that new books can be added whenever they come in and we can find the one we want whenever we want.

If the books were not organized this way and instead were put on the shelves in the chronological order they arrived at the library, like how we experience things in life, it would make finding the one we wanted almost impossible. This is why we may need time to process new information, so we can organize our experiences to make them easier to understand and retrieve them when we need them.

Interpretation.

The law of shared meaning motivates us to interpret information by investing it with meaning. When we interpret information we can make comparisons between the new information and the information we already know.

Interpretation of information is important because it has the potential to change our perceptions. This can affect how we communicate with others, our behavior, and how we see ourselves. Generally, our perceptions do not suddenly or significantly change our social reality because we need consistency.

Consistency increases stability and reduces uncertainty, which makes us better able to function. However, there must be a way to change and adapt our perceptions in order to utilize new information. This can create tension between what we know and what we perceive, which can lead to internal conflict.

Our past perceptions and interpretations influence how we make sense of new information. We tend to look for things that are familiar to us because they fit in with what we already know.

Interpretation of new information can take time and energy. This is why when something unexpected, shocking, or traumatic happens we may need time to come to terms with it. We need time to process our experience and new information because it may not easily fit in with our past experiences or what we already know. It is helpful at these times to allow yourself the time to process information or experiences to deal with them as well as possible.

Our mood or emotional state can affect how receptive we are to new information as well as how we interpret it. We have a tendency to be more perceptive when we are experiencing uncertainty because it motivates us to look for something new or different to improve our circumstances.

When uncertainty is reduced, we tend to be more satisfied with our situation and less likely to look for something new as there is less motivation to change. Alternately, people who are overly dissatisfied such as being upset or angry might reject new information because they are not able to handle it at the time.

Perception causes us to form impressions of people. When we meet someone we have limited information about them. The perception process compares what we observe to our past experiences and then we fill in the gaps to form an impression of others.

There are many factors that influence the perception process. Consider what factors influence your perception. Doing this can be helpful to increase your awareness of not only how the process works, but how you select, interpret, organize, and use information to help you to communicate more effectively.

Expectations

We have expectations about ourselves, others, and practically everything around us. Without expectations, we could not function in everyday life because they allow us to do things without having to think about them.

We are motivated by the law of uncertainty to develop expectations so we have a reasonable idea of what things will be like in the future. Expectations reduce uncertainty by providing a measure of how well we are doing. If our perception of reality matches or exceeds expectation, we feel good about things. If they do not, it can make us feel frustrated, upset, or even angry.

Expectations fulfill the law of shared meaning because they give things additional meaning. Expectations make the law of investing work because without having reasonable expectations of getting a return, we would be reluctant to invest our time and energy in anything. This means that expectations often represent benefits we would like to receive in the future.

Expectations may be realistic or unrealistic, accurate or off base, but we could not function without them. When we do something for others, we cannot be sure what they will actually do in return. Without reasonable expectations of some type of reciprocation or benefit, people would not be as willing to invest their time, energy, money, and other resources in the things that are important for society to function.

We have expectations about practically all aspects of our life including what we do, what others do, our family, our friends, our job, our coworkers, and what life should be like. There are many things that we need to do to get through everyday life that would not be possible without expectations.

For example, we expect to wake up in the morning and get ready for work. At work we expect everything to be as we left it and to get certain tasks done. After work we expect to go home, have dinner, and go to bed.

Our day is full of many of these small expectations. We don't think much about them because most of the time they are fulfilled. However, when our expectations are not realized, it can be a source of dissatisfaction, tension, and even conflict.

Most of the time everything goes well, so we become accustomed to having these expectations met. However, when they do not go as we expect, it can throw us making us feel frustrated or angry. The smaller the expectation, the more likely we are to expect it to happen. This can be one reason why may people blow up over small, seemingly insignificant things.

We obey the rules of society because we expect to have our needs and wants fulfilled. If we did not have these expectations, we would be less likely to accept the rules of social reality.

The perception and expectation gap.

Our feelings of satisfaction can have a lot to do with the gap between our perception of reality and our expectations. Success can be seen as the difference between our expectations of need and want fulfillment and our perception of what we receive. For example, when our perception of reality exceeds our expectations we are likely to feel happy, even elated at our accomplishments.

Conversely, when our perception of reality is below our expectations, we can feel upset, unhappy, or even angry. In each case, the gap between our perceptions and expectations creates tangible feelings and emotions that can affect our behavior and actions. Our behavior can be markedly different depending upon if we feel successful or not based upon our perceptions and expectations.

Everyone's perception of reality is different and so are their expectations. A person with a seemingly high degree of success might be dissatisfied based upon the gap between their perceptions and expectations. This may be one reason why people who seem successful can be unhappy.

It may be because their perception of reality does not meet their expectations. Conversely, people who may not be considered as successful can be happier, because their perceptions meet their expectations.

Managing expectations.

We have expectations that things should get better over time. If our perceptions don't meet our expectations, it can be frustrating or debilitating. It can even make us quit trying altogether. If our perceptions exceed our expectations, we may feel that everything is fine and may not do anything to improve ourselves.

In order to make improvements, it can be helpful to have expectations slightly above your perceptions to help motivate sustained improvement. When your expectations are slightly above your perceptions they can seem more achievable.

If our expectations are too big it can become discouraging and if they are too small there won't be much improvement. So, in order to use perceptions and expectations to motivate behavior, set your expectations just enough above your perceptions to motivate you to improve without being discouraging.

What expectations do you have about yourself, your family, your job, your co-workers, or your life? It can be helpful to think about your perceptions and expectations. Ask yourself if your perceptions are accurate or not. Ask yourself if your expectations are realistic or not.

Tension, unhappiness, and even conflict can come from inaccurate perceptions and unrealistic expectations. By understanding your perceptions and expectations, you can determine how accurate they are and if they are a source of unnecessary unhappiness. Sometimes clarifying perceptions and expectations can make them more realistic improving your outlook on life.

We all have expectations and make judgments based on our perceptions. It's a natural part of how we reduce uncertainty. We do this so often they become second nature, so we don't think much about them until they become a problem. By being aware of our expectations, we can be more realistic about what we expect of ourselves and others.

Awareness

Awareness is about how we gather information through the perception process, and how we use that information gives us options. Awareness is something we do naturally without thinking much about it. We feel that we are aware of what's around us because we notice things every day, however, awareness is a skill that can be developed.

Awareness involves developing our perception process so that we notice more of what is around us. It helps us to interpret and organize the information we perceive. It is the ability to look at what you know and use it in new ways.

Awareness includes self-awareness, which is knowing what we are communicating both verbally and nonverbally to others and how they perceive us. It includes being aware of our own style of communicating including how our perceptions and expectations influence our behavior.

Increasing self-awareness can be difficult because we don't know what we don't know. So, it can be helpful to see yourself as others see you. The interference of The Great Abyss can limit or constrain our self-awareness.

Everyone can improve their awareness skills utilizing everyday activities. For example, if you are sitting in a restaurant, coffee shop, at work, or just about anywhere, take a minute and close your eyes. Try to remember everything you can about your surroundings. What people are in the room? What do they look like? What is the room like? What kind of furniture is in it and where is it located? Then open your eyes and see how accurate you were.

The purpose is to train your mind to be naturally aware of your surroundings. This can help you to communicate more effectively, have a greater understanding of yourself and others, and in extreme situations might save your life. For example, could you describe someone to the police if you had to identify them?

Could you find your way out of the room or building if you could not see, if the electricity went out, or there was smoke from a fire? Developing these skills can give us confidence and competence in our own abilities.

Options

Increasing our awareness can provide us with more options and having options helps us communicate more effectively. Having options is not just about having choices, but having the ability to choose the best one in a given situation.

Having options can help us to not fall into the habit of doing the same things over and over when they may not be effective. It helps us to evaluate our ways of doing things to see what can be improved to be more effective. The more options you have, the better your chances are of achieving your desired outcome.

However, options are good up to a point, because having too many can be as problematic as too few. When we have too many options, we can become paralyzed with an inability to choose one. Most of the time we need only a few good choices.

Awareness helps us to look at what works and why it works. Having awareness and options makes it possible for you to change or add new ideas and skills, so you can choose what works best for you.

Communicating Skills

Confidence and competence.

To effectively communicate with others, it is helpful to have confidence and competence. Confidence is about our believing in ourselves, our skills, and our abilities. It is the ability to develop our own self-image and control how we present it to others. It is the ability to choose how we communicate with others so that they will understand us and respond positively to us. It is the ability to communicate effectively to achieve your desired outcomes.

People who speak clearly and with authority, who are knowledgeable, and are aware of themselves and others as well as the situation are often perceived as being confident. People are more likely to be receptive to someone who shows confidence because it makes them feel safe and secure by reducing uncertainty.

Competence is having a variety of skills and the ability to use them effectively. It is having an awareness of our own skills and knowledge of the options that are available to us. These skills can be based upon our experiences, education, and expertise.

Practicing these skills not only makes us better at them, it makes us more confident so we will be perceived by others as being more competent. People who are competent are seen as being more likable, organized, and professional. Having competence gives us the confidence to use our knowledge and skills to the best of our ability.

Range and repertoire.

Range is the variety of notes produced by a musician, the area in which something can operate, or the distance something can travel. In communicating, range is the variety of skills you have to communicate effectively with people in many different types of situations.

In music, repertoire is the body of artistic works a musician is able to perform. In communicating, it can be the variety of resources, techniques, or skills available to communicate effectively with others.

This gives you options and having options gives you the flexibility and freedom to make choices rather than reacting to the actions of others. Having range and repertoire provides a variety of choices to make the right one for your particular situation.

Adaptability and performance.

Adaptability is having the expertise and ability to apply a variety of options and select the one that works best in a given situation. It's having the flexibility to move from one option to another until a successful one is found.

Performance is having the expertise and capability to use communicating skills in real situations to communicate more effectively. Performance skills are developed through practice and experience.

People who are effective communicators have the ability to adapt and hone their approach to communicate differently based on the situation and individuals involved. To do this it's helpful to break out of familiar patterns, to try new approaches, and to be aware of the feedback we receive from others.

Individual Communicating

Do you ever talk to yourself? We communicate with ourselves in many ways. It may be out loud, it may be listening to our inner voice, or simply thinking inside our head. However it happens, we are constantly communicating with ourselves sending messages like, "I feel good today," or "Why did I say that," or "I feel so embarrassed."

These messages are often about how we feel about ourselves or our perceptions about what is happening around us. We do this in order to help understand what we perceive.

Individual communicating is about you. It is about how you communicate with yourself. Our self-concept is in part developed based on how we communicate with ourselves and the kinds of messages we send. This is why it can be helpful to increase our awareness of the messages we send ourselves, so we can be in control of them in order to improve our self-concept.

So, why do we communicate with ourselves? Doing this helps us to organize our thoughts and sort out the information we receive. We do it to reduce uncertainty and learn more about ourselves, to help understand our experiences by giving them meaning, and to invest in ourselves. It is how we process information to make it useful to us. It helps us to make good decisions by weighing our options and thinking things through.

Our perceptions create expectations and we can develop expectations by what we tell ourselves. For example, you may tell yourself that you should have better relationships or more time for yourself. Eventually, you may begin to believe these expectations and act based upon them whether they are accurate or not.

By increasing our awareness of the messages that we send ourselves, we can make choices about what types of messages to send and which types to avoid. This gives us options to make choices about how we communicate with ourselves instead of falling into the same patterns. We can then choose to send ourselves more positive messages that can help improve how we perceive ourselves.

Self-Concept

Our self-concept is how we think about ourselves based on our perceptions and expectations. We develop our self-concept by communicating with ourselves and others. Our self-concept can be positive or negative depending upon the types of messages we receive.

For example, if we tell ourselves that we did a good job, it can bolster our self-concept and people are more likely to perceive us as more confident. When they do, they may treat us in a positive way reinforcing this self-concept. When other people like our friends, family, or coworkers tell us we've done a good job, it can bolster our self-concept so we see ourselves in a positive way. This is how perception can affect how we act, if others perceive us as more confident it can make their perception a reality.

Conversely, if we tell ourselves negative messages like we don't feel that we know what we are doing, others may pick up on our lack of confidence. They may perceive us as lacking ability, which can have a negative impact on our self-concept.

How we communicate can have real and tangible consequences, so perceptions can become a reality. Sometimes if we hear messages long enough, we may eventually come to believe that they are true becoming a part of how we see ourselves.

Developing your self-concept is about getting to know yourself, which can be one of the great adventures in life. If we had a total understanding of ourselves there would be little motivation for self-discovery, personal growth, or self-improvement, which would make life less interesting. Instead, we are motivated to know more about ourselves by looking for meaning in ourselves and in our experiences.

How self-concept is created.

Our self-concept is the picture that we have of ourselves in our mind consisting of our perceptions and expectations. It develops slowly over time and as we get older becomes more stable and resistant to change.

The perception process helps us to gather, select, organize, and interpret information other people send us to construct a picture of how we look to them. Some of this information we keep and some we discard. We are more likely to keep information that fits in with how we perceive ourselves and discard things that contradict our perceptions, whether they are accurate or not. The information that we keep becomes a part of our self-concept and how we see ourselves.

This is one reason why the way others respond to us can be helpful or hurtful to our self-concept. If we receive positive feedback, we feel good about ourselves. Conversely, if we receive negative feedback it can hurt our self-concept and make us feel bad about ourselves.

This is why it's important to be around people who are supportive and to avoid those who are overly negative because of the effect it can have on us and our self-concept.

While feedback can affect our self-concept, by being aware of how it works we can decide how we want to use it. When people provide feedback they may consciously or subconsciously wait to see if we accept it or not. If we accept it, it may confirm how they perceive us. If we reject it or correct their perception, they may be open to changing their perception of us.

While it shouldn't matter what other people think about us, the reality is that it does. It matters because if people like us then we feel good about ourselves and that we are a good person because people like other people who are good.

Instead of using feedback, we could develop a more accurate self-concept through self-awareness. We could utilize objective criteria based upon the things we do. However, that would be more difficult and time consuming. So we use feedback from other people because it's so easy to do we often don't notice it.

There are people and things in life that give us energy and make us feel rejuvenated. These include doing things that we like to do, being places we like to be, and being around people we like. However, we may feel full of energy and then for no apparent reason feel drained. This is because there are also things that drain our energy making us feel tired and frustrated.

It can be helpful to increase our awareness of what gives and takes energy from us. This can provide options on how we could maximize those things that give us energy and reduce those that take it from us.

Communicating with others and receiving feedback is not the only means by which we develop our self-concept. We also do this by comparing ourselves to other people like our family members, friends, coworkers, neighbors, even famous people. We consciously and subconsciously compare ourselves to these people to see how we are doing.

How we form our self-concept is an example of how we compare our perception of reality to our expectations. It creates a picture of ourselves where we might measure up or fall short. It can be based upon accurate or unrealistic information.

This can affect how we behave around others. If our perceptions and expectations are realistic and are fairly close to each other, we can feel more confident helping us to be successful in what we do.

If our perception is overly negative or if we have unrealistic expectations, we may feel inadequate so we act in ways that are less likely to be successful in what we do. In this way perceptions can create reality.

Self-concept and expectations.

Our self-concept can also be affected by how well our expectations match our perceptions based upon feedback from others. Perceptions and expectations are intangible qualities that exist in our mind, but can create physical reality. They can influence how we communicate with ourselves affecting our behavior.

Our perceptions can differ from actual reality creating an inaccurate, even distorted view of ourselves. Part of our self-concept can be based upon the difference between our perceptions and expectations because we have expectations about ourselves and how we want others to perceive us.

If the feedback we receive meets or exceeds our expectations it can create a positive self-concept, feelings of self-worth, and increased confidence. If the feedback does not meet our expectations we may become frustrated, upset, and even angry. This can be influenced in part by our perception of reality being significantly different from the actual reality that others perceive.

Perception of our self-concept can be self-perpetuating because we communicate with others based upon how we see ourselves. This can affect our behavior and how we communicate with them. Others perceive this behavior and may interpret it similar to how we perceive ourselves. They respond appropriately based upon their perception and interpretation of our behavior. Then the response we receive can verify our perception of ourselves.

Most of the time these perceptions reflect reality, but if they don't, the positive ones can cancel out the negative creating a balance. However, we can get into cycles where we have an inaccurate self-concept that others perceive and reflect back to us reinforcing a distorted perspective. If we are unaware that this is happening, it could cause our self-concept to inflate unrealistically or diminish needlessly giving us a false sense of who we are.

If we have an overly negative perception of ourselves, we may send overly negative messages that are then reflected back to us. We may receive both positive and negative messages, but only pay attention to the negative ones. Positive messages might be filtered out by The Great Abyss or we may not even look for them because we do not expect them.

This creates a negative cycle that can be difficult to break. Through awareness, we can check the messages that we are getting and use other information to develop our self-concept in order to take control of the process and break the cycle.

Our perceptions can also create a reality that affects our self-concept. We constantly form expectations based upon our perceptions in order to function in everyday life. We have expectations that we communicate to others. So, we look for information to fulfill expectations through the process of communicating.

We may filter out information that does not support our expectations because we are not necessarily looking for it. Our perceptions are based upon the information we perceive, so our expectations now become a part of our set of perceptions.

This information can confirm our expectations and become part of our perception of reality. If we believe these perceptions to be true, we can take action based upon them whether they are accurate or not. By taking action we may actually make these perceptions a reality.

For instance, if we are in a relationship and have the expectation that our partner will breakup with us, we look for evidence to support that expectation. If we do not look for evidence to the contrary, everything we perceive may be interpreted as supporting our expectation because we might filter out anything that contradicts it. This can turn our expectations into perceptions. It could motivate us to breakup with them, even though they never wanted to do so.

Having an awareness of how we create our self-concept can help us to avoid distorted information that can be harmful to us. If we receive feedback that is negative or overly critical, it can contribute needlessly to a poor self-image.

If we receive information that is overly positive, it can give us an inflated sense of ourselves encouraging arrogance. Being overly confident can be harmful because it makes us resistant to feedback that could be beneficial to us.

It's helpful to be aware of this process because having a positive self-concept has many benefits. People who have a positive self-concept are generally more respectful of others, work harder, and strive for higher standards. They look realistically at their abilities and want to improve themselves.

They are not overly critical of others and take criticism without feeling a need to defend themselves. They are comfortable trying new things and taking risks. They are comfortable complementing others and giving them credit for their accomplishments.

People who have a negative self-concept tend to think less of others and themselves. They tend to do less and do not try to meet higher standards. They may have a tendency to defend themselves against criticism and are uncomfortable sharing ideas with others who may not agree with them. They may take the safe approach by being unwilling to take risks or try new things.

We can have a natural tendency to focus on the negative more than on what is positive. This is not because we are overly pessimistic, it's because negativity increases uncertainty making us uncomfortable, so it gets our attention. We may pay less attention to things that are positive because they are less likely to get through the interference of The Great Abyss than something negative.

When something goes well the tension is resolved making it more comfortable reducing uncertainty, so it is less likely to get our attention. When something is negative it is unresolved, so it creates tension that gets our attention. Because it is uncomfortable it cuts through the interference, until we do something about it.

When it comes to our self-concept, we are more likely to be motivated to look for information that confirms how we already perceive ourselves. We might put ourselves in situations and spend time around other people who will confirm our self-concept. We do this because their confirmation is a form of acceptance that is a social reward. When others confirm what we already know, we feel that we are right and we would rather be right than wrong.

When we come across information that contradicts what we feel we already know, it can create tension increasing uncertainty that can make us uncomfortable. This tension must be resolved by either changing what we already know or dismissing the new information. It can be easier to dismiss new information than to change what we know because it feels safe and secure.

We have a natural tendency to seek out information from relationships with others who confirm our current self-concept. We might reject others who have a different perception of our self-concept even if it is more accurate or more positive.

We do this because we develop a mindset that information contrary to what we already know will not make a difference because it will not change who we are.

It can be easier to rationalize or justify the current situation than to change it. It can sometimes be easier to attack anyone who challenges our perceptions then to change them.

It can be difficult to break out of a negative self-concept because we are motivated to confirm what we think we already know. It can help to understand how this process works to get more accurate feedback from others and take advantage of naturally occurring change.

We can seek out feedback from people who are positive and supportive of us, and avoid being around those who are negative. We can increase our awareness and seek out more accurate information for a more realistic view of ourselves. Doing this can help us develop a desire to change and a willingness to work at it.

Developing an awareness of how we create and maintain our self-concept can help us to have control over how we perceive ourselves rather than having it control us. Most of the time this process works without having to think too much about it making it easy for negative and inaccurate information to become part of how we see ourselves.

Not all feedback we receive should be considered when it comes to our self-concept. We should protect ourselves from others who are overly negative or critical and information that could damage how we see ourselves.

We should seek out feedback from people we trust, who are honest, and who are supportive of us. We can reduce or eliminate relationships where we receive negative feedback that can damage our self-esteem. We can develop a process of awareness and self-monitoring so that we can form our own criteria for evaluating ourselves to rely more on our own perceptions and less on the opinions of others.

By utilizing awareness and options we can create a more realistic and balanced self-image that is acceptable to us. This can help us to have better self-esteem and a more accurate self-concept.

Evaluating self-concept.

It can be helpful to evaluate your self-concept and how you developed it by making an inventory of your strengths, weaknesses, accomplishments, and areas you would like to improve. Writing them down helps to validate the information you have to see how accurate or relevant it is.

You might discover that your self-concept is based on outdated information and experiences that happened long ago. Negative experiences tend to stay longer in our memory even when they may no longer be relevant. This is because they represent unresolved tension, which is uncomfortable so it gets our attention.

The purpose of doing this is to create a more realistic picture of yourself. Doing this can help to form your own self-concept relying less on information from other people. By having realistic expectations based on clear perceptions of yourself, you can recognize your strengths while putting your weaknesses in perspective

Doing this can help to change an outdated or negative self-concept, which can help you feel better about yourself and improve your relationships with others.

We all have a picture in our mind of the person we want to be. We want to improve ourselves to reach that ideal picture, however, we often get sidetracked by everyday responsibilities such as work, family, and the hundreds of other things that use up our time and energy. This can make it difficult for us to find time for self-improvement.

People change for basically one of two reasons, they want to change or they have to change. Most of the time we do the things we need or have to do. All too often we never get to the things we want or ought to do. Good intentions like making plans are no substitute for actually doing something.

It's important to have the resources and support to make necessary changes. Change is difficult because it involves hard work, even though it can be rewarding. Meaningful change must come from within ourselves by deciding that we are going to change. And isn't it better to change because we want to, rather than waiting until we have to change?

In order to reduce uncertainty we need to be able to open our mind to new ideas, new ways of doing things, and think about what we already know in a new or different way.

This can be one of the most challenging things we do because the law of uncertainty creates tension between change and stability. We can find our own way to balance these tensions in order to consider new ideas.

We can do this by developing a way to add new information to what we already know without undermining it. This can be difficult to do because we are busy doing everyday tasks that need to be done, so we don't always have the time or energy to think about new things.

By setting aside some time to process the information we take in, we can consider possibilities we might otherwise overlook or discard.

Typically, when we have something we need to do we set out to do it. Along the way opportunities may present themselves, but we may not be open to them. We might reduce uncertainty to the point where we become focused on just getting things done.

This can prevent us from perceiving new information that may be around us. We may not consider other options until something happens to increase uncertainty motivating us to do so.

By understanding the law of uncertainty, we can develop ways to initiate this process when we want to, before we are forced to do it. By increasing awareness, we can utilize the perception process to be more receptive to new information.

We can utilize the process of communicating by understanding how others communicate their Great Idea to make connections with us, so that we can make choices about our frame of reference and what to filter out. By being aware of how we can use the perception process, we can have more options to communicate more effectively with others.

Developing creativity.

An important skill to be successful in business is the ability to be creative. Creativity involves more than just our ability to evaluate existing information, it is about our ability to use our imagination to make something new and original. It helps us to use our resources in new and different ways to solve problems and make decisions.

We use creativity to reduce uncertainty because it fosters innovation, develops new ideas, and creates new things. It is a means to find new ways to understand the world around us. We use it to reduce uncertainty about ourselves through self-expression.

Because creativity often involves things that are new and unfamiliar, it has a certain amount of inherent uncertainty that could make some people reluctant to be creative or appreciate the creativity of others.

Creativity is a means by which we share meaning about ourselves, others, and the world around us. Creativity utilizes the many types of connections we make with others. It helps us to share meaning that transcends language and culture in ways few other things do.

For instance, we can understand music and appreciate art created by people from other cultures, as well as from other periods in history even if we know little else about them. We don't necessarily have to understand them to appreciate their creativity.

We use creativity to invest things with meaning by investing our time, energy, and self-concept in them. Often when we create something such as a work of art, it represents an investment of ourselves and our self-concept that we communicate to others. When people share meanings with others through creativity they may add to social reality.

We use creativity to fulfill many of our needs and wants. The creative expression of others helps us fulfill our need for entertainment, excitement, adventure, and something new.

We have a need to communicate our unique individuality through creative expression. When we are creative it fulfills our need for self-expression, self-fulfillment, to earn an income, and to make life more enjoyable.

Creativity is a means to make connections with others to communicate our Great Idea. How others respond through the process of communicating works as feedback that can affect our self-concept.

This may be why we are at times reluctant to share our creativity due to uncertainty about how others will receive it. If they like it, it bolsters our self-concept. If they do not, it can hurt our self-concept undermining our confidence.

Just what we consider creative can depend on our perceptions and expectations. We perceive things as being creative based on our past experiences, culture, education, and other factors. What is creative to one person may not be to others.

Our perceptions create expectations about what it means to be creative. When we think of creativity we often think of the arts. However, creativity doesn't have to be just artistic expression, it can be part of any aspect of our lives. Creativity is less about what we do and more about how we do it.

To be creative, start with what you like, what you are interested in, or what you feel passionate about. Creativity is like other communicating skills, it can be developed over time. By developing your ideas, increasing your awareness, and exploring options for self-expression you can foster your creativity.

Ask for feedback from people you trust, who will provide objective feedback, and who will be supportive. While it is nice to have people tell us how wonderful we are, it's more useful to have them give us specific information we can utilize to improve our skills.

Creativity involves seeing and doing things that are familiar in new and different ways. By going beyond normal traditional ways of thinking we can create innovation, increase productivity, and improve our quality of life.

We might feel reluctant to be creative for fear others may judge or reject us. We might feel that others are better than we are and we will not look good.

But that shouldn't stop you from being creative. Creativity is expressing your unique individuality because only you can be you.

Time Management

One of the most important skills in business is time management. Time is our most valuable resource because it is our most limited one. While we all have different amounts of resources available to us like money or space, we all have the same twenty four hours each day. We can make more money, but we cannot make more time. So, managing time effectively is an important skill.

How we spend time communicates a great deal about us including our interests, priorities, values, and who we are.

Since time is our most limited resource it creates value. We might judge the value of things by the time that we put in to them. We value relationships where we spend time and we spent time in relationships we value. Because our time is limited we cannot spend it on everything we want to, so we have to make choices and set priorities. These choices communicate what is important to us.

What we do with our time is an observable way to measure values and priorities. We might say something is important, however, we may spend little or no time on it communicating a different message.

When we spend a lot of time on something, we have expectations of what we want to get in return. For instance, we spend a large amount of time at our jobs so we expect to be compensated fairly for it.

Punctuality is about being on time and it is important because of what it communicates about us and how we perceive others. Being punctual can be perceived as a sign of respect and courtesy. When someone is late, people may become offended because they think you are wasting their time, whether it's intentional or not.

Effective communicating is a matter of having appropriate timing. There are times when people are more receptive to your message and times when they are less receptive. By increasing your awareness you can use timing to tactfully communicate information. Timing can make the difference between being accepted or rejected. It is important to choose an appropriate time and place to communicate to achieve your desired outcome

It can be helpful to take an assessment of how you are spending your time to increase your awareness of what you may be communicating to others because perception can be different than reality. For instance, we may feel that we may be spending enough time with our family or coworkers when in reality we are not meeting their expectations.

It seems that we never have enough time to fulfill all our needs and wants. This means we have to make choices and set priorities, which can create tension between conflicting needs and wants. This can mean that we spend most of our time on more pressing short term needs putting off long term wants because we feel that we will find time for them later.

This can leave us feeling frustrated or unhappy and wondering why. By understanding how we spend our time and what that communicates to others, we can increase our awareness to give ourselves more options to balance how we use our time relieving tension and reducing frustration. The first step can be to understand how accurately your perceptions and expectations reflect reality.

Do you feel that you have enough time each day to get everything done you need to do? Do you feel that your time could be better spent?

In order to more effectively utilize your time, from memory write down on a piece of paper everything you have done in the last month. Next to each item write down how much time you think you spent doing each one.

Now take your calendar and look to see how much time you actually spent doing these things. This will tell you how accurate your perception of how you use your time is, because perception can be different than reality.

On another piece of paper, write down each thing you want to do during the next month and how much time you want to spend on each one. Then put that list away where you won't see it.

For the next month, keep a detailed calendar of what you do and how much time you actually spend on each item. After the month is over, compare your calendar to the list you wrote at the beginning of the month to see how it compares. This will tell you how accurate your perceptions and expectations are so you can adjust your time to how you want to spend it.

In organizing your time it can be helpful to consider these four kinds of needs and wants.

1. What you need to do. These are things you must do in order to live.
2. What you have to do. These are everyday things you do, but could live without.
3. What you want to do. These are fun things to do that make you feel good.
4. What you ought to do. These are the things you know you should do.

Life would be much easier if we could do all of these tasks all the time. Since we have limited resources, making choices can be a source of conflict because doing one thing can preclude us from doing others.

For instance, imagine it's Sunday morning and you need to get groceries, have to clean the house, ought to go to church, and want to sleep in. You must be at work by noon, so you cannot do all of them. Which one do you choose?

In order to communicate effectively with others, it's helpful to be aware of just how we are actually spending our time and what that communicates to them.

By increasing your awareness, you can see how you are actually spending your time. It's easy for time to get away and be spent in ways you do not want or intend to do. So, doing an audit and creating a budget of your time can help to organize the things that you do based on both short and long term priorities. This can help you to use your time more effectively in order to achieve your desired outcomes.

Once we are aware of how we spend our time and how we want to use it, we can take action to make changes to use it more effectively. While we may think about doing this, actually writing it down on paper helps to clarify our perceptions, so we can have realistic expectations. By evaluating how we are actually spending our time, we can reduce uncertainty to have more control over how we spend it.

Leaders and Leadership

A leader is a specific role that is created within a group of people. It can be the most important role because a leader has power and influence over the other members of a group.

Leaders can be responsible for managing the group, assigning tasks, regulating norms, allocating resources, and enforcing the rules. Businesses and organizations have different types of leaders that gain their position by a variety of means.

Leaders can be chosen through the process of behavior reinforcement. Since the leader is such an important role it may be the most difficult one for the group to select. If two or more members want to be leaders or the group is unable to select a leader, it can hurt the effectiveness of the group.

People find leaders attractive. They not only aspire to be leaders, they like to be around them. Perhaps it's because this fulfills the need for status, prestige, or to feel important even if they are only around others who are important. It may fulfill a need to have power or exert influence over others. It could be to fulfill a need to receive the social and material benefits that leaders can provide.

Even though we find leaders attractive, people often deny that they want to be a leader. This may be because society can be suspicious of its leaders. People who want to run for public office often deny they want to run until the last moment and when they do, they claim that they are running for the good of the people, not for themselves.

There is no one best way to become a group leader. Becoming a leader depends upon gaining the support of the other group members. If you want to be a leader you have to act like one and make connections with the other group members.

Leaders show up, arrive early, stay late, and don't miss meetings. One of the simplest things you can do is show up. Few things irritate people more than someone who shows up late, leaves early, or misses meetings. To be a leader it takes commitment and dedication to the group above and beyond what is expected of other members.

Leaders talk appropriately contributing to the group discussion. Do not dominate the conversation, but do not hold back either. Keep what you say simple, easy to understand, straightforward, and nonjudgmental. When others speak actually listen to them and show support for what they have to say. Ask questions and offer your opinion at the appropriate time.

Leaders provide positive feedback to the other members because it bolsters their self-concept. Be polite and supportive of other people's ideas. It makes them feel good so they will like being a member.

Leaders are serious. Joking around and being the center of attention may get people to laugh or to like you, but they are not likely to take you seriously as a leader.

Leaders do their homework, gather information, and are prepared. People who are perceived as knowledgeable have a greater chance of becoming a leader. Group members need to know what they can expect from a leader and a leader needs to know what they can expect from the other group members.

People join groups to reduce uncertainty and leaders can help make the group more stable and secure. They help keep the group on task to achieve its desired outcomes.

Leaders help allocate resources so group members can have their needs and wants fulfilled. They can create a feeling of security to instill confidence in the group by being supportive, helpful, fair, and by doing what they say they are going to do.

Leaders provide information, allocate resources, and assign tasks so group members can do their work more effectively. They help make plans for the future and follow up to see that things get done. They help structure the group and its procedures to work more effectively to make good use of its resources like each member's time.

Leaders delegate responsibility, so that everyone does their fair share and they allocate benefits so everyone feels they benefit fairly. They help the group to make decisions by encouraging everyone to participate, so that they feel they are contributing to the group.

Leaders help the group solve problems, work out disagreements, and resolve conflicts. They do this to help increase member satisfaction and commitment to the group.

Leaders can encourage self-disclosure to develop social relationships, so that group members feel comfortable with one another enabling them to work together more effectively. They can help members feel that they are making a contribution and that they are valued as an important part of the group.

Leaders help members feel like they fit in with the group and introduce new members to the others so they feel comfortable. They can lead the group in rituals and traditions that shares meaning within the group. They can help members understand the history and significance of the group and what it means to be a member.

Leaders communicate the big picture and a vision of the future, so that group members know where they fit in, where they are going, and what to expect in the future.

Leaders encourage investment in the group and its members. It is important to create and maintain the stability of the group by helping to develop rules and fairly enforce them. They help the group to be able to create an atmosphere of trust so members can invest their time and other resources in the group.

Leaders see that everyone benefits from the group and receives fair rewards for fair contributions. They help encourage longevity of the group for its members, so they are comfortable investing in the group over long periods of time. They maintain connections outside the group to help bring in information and other resources the group needs.

Leaders encourage members to participate in decision making giving them a feeling of ownership in the group process, so that they are more likely to support and implement decisions.

Leaders set an example to get other members of the group to invest in the well being of the group by putting the interests of the group above their own. They give credit to other members and reward them for what they do. They help to elevate the status and prestige of others and don't worry about getting credit for themselves, but rather share it with others.

Leaders bring out leadership qualities in others by helping them to develop their competence and bolster their confidence. They are not threatened by the successes of others, but rather compliment their accomplishments and achievements.

Leaders help fulfill needs and wants. We join groups to receive benefits that fulfill our needs and wants. Since leaders often allocate many of these benefits they have influence over the behavior of the other members.

Leaders can use their influence for the benefit of the group by helping members to get things done. They can provide benefits for those who do well. By providing benefits, leaders help to increase member satisfaction and increase commitment by making the group attractive. Leaders help to recruit new members to the group and help them to learn the rules of the group by providing information or serving as a mentor to help them fit in.

Leaders shape perceptions and expectations. Everyone has expectations about what a leader should be and what they should do. Leaders can help the group by managing the perceptions and expectations of its members. They can clearly communicate their perceptions so that group members have realistic expectations of them as well as of themselves.

Leaders can provide current and accurate information about the group and what is happening around them to help keep the perceptions of their members in line with reality. There can be a tendency for leaders to portray things better than they really are so that others will like them and follow them.

They may do this if they are fearful that by being honest they may lose the group's support. However, by being truthful, but tactful they can help the group to create accurate perceptions and realistic expectations.

Leaders can be more effective when they have an awareness of their own style of communicating, the style of their members, and the style of outsiders. They need to have an awareness of what is going on both inside the group and outside the group that affects it.

Leaders communicate a vision of the future to help shape expectations, so that everyone will work together for the same desired outcomes. This can help motivate the members to invest in the group over the long term, so they will work toward making that vision a reality.

Leaders communicate the big picture to the group, so that everyone knows how they fit in and how they contribute to the whole. People are more committed to groups and organizations when they understand the big picture, know how they fit in, and can see that they make a difference.

All too often we do not see the big picture or know where we fit in creating a sense that what we do does not matter. By seeing the big picture, people can feel that they are part of something bigger than themselves and what they do matters because they are making a difference. This helps increase individual member's satisfaction and commitment to the group.

Chapter 5
Creating Great Relationships

What if you had to move away from where you live now to a place where you didn't know anyone?

What if you had to leave behind everyone you know including your family, friends, neighbors, and coworkers, and not have any contact with them? What would you do?

Throughout our life we are constantly meeting new people and developing new relationships while others fade away. While we will probably not have to make all new relationships at the same time, thinking about this possibility can help us better understand how we have developed the ones we have now.

This process is such a natural part of life we usually don't pay attention to it because we are constantly going through the process of forming, maintaining, and ending relationships. So, what would you do if you had to form all new relationships?

Creating relationships.

In business, developing relationships can be difficult. People seem to do things for no apparent reason. We might feel that things are not going right or did not turn out like we wanted. This can leave us feeling upset or frustrated and we may not know why.

By understanding how the laws of uncertainty, shared meaning, and investing affect us, we can better understand how relationships are created and maintained. We can develop skills to communicate effectively with others to improve our relationships. People may say, it's not personal it's just business. However, even in business, when it comes to relationships with people, it's always personal.

Think about the people you communicate with each and every day. Who are they? Where did you meet them? What do you talk about? Perhaps you know them socially as friends, professionally as coworkers, or intimately as family members.

Each of these is a different type of connection that varies from impersonal to intimate. The ongoing patterns of communicating through connections that are recognized by both people determine the nature of the relationship.

We are motivated to form relationships to help us fulfill needs and wants we cannot fulfill ourselves. We enjoy being around other people like our friends and family. However, there can be times when we feel like we are struggling or working harder in a relationship than we should.

There can be times when things don't feel quite right and we're not sure why. By understanding how we create and maintain relationships, we can increase our awareness of what is happening in them. This gives us options to improve them, so we can feel better about them. We can reduce uncertainty to help us share meaning, so that we can invest in relationships with others and they will invest in us.

We are motivated to form relationships by the law of uncertainty. When we don't know someone there is a high degree of uncertainty because we don't know what to expect from them. They probably feel the same because they do not know what to expect from us.

When we reduce uncertainty we create security and stability making it easier for us to communicate with them. This builds trust making it easier for us to develop a relationship with them. This process is important because if we didn't get to know people and develop relationships with them, it would be nearly impossible to work together to get things done.

We are motivated by the law of investing to invest our time and other resources in others in order to fulfill our needs and wants. The more we get to know someone, and the more they get to know us, the more likely we are to be comfortable investing in relationships with them. This is because when we get to know them we have reasonable expectations of their behavior creating stability and predictability.

In relationships, we get to know what to expect from others and they get to know what they can expect from us. We are willing to make investments with the expectation of receiving fair rewards. We invest in relationships based upon our future expectations.

In the process of communicating, you create your Great Idea and communicate it to others across The Great Abyss. You do this by making connections with them. When you make a connection directly with another person, it may constitute the beginning of a relationship. This is because you have established your place in "relation" to the other person. If the connection is reciprocated, a relationship can be created.

Rules govern how people in a relationship communicate with one another as well as regulating their behavior. When others fulfill our expectations, we are more likely to reciprocate and follow the rules because they enable us to fulfill our needs and wants. When our perceptions of others do not meet our expectations, we are more likely to challenge or reject the rules because we may feel that they inhibit us from achieving our desired outcome.

When we first meet someone our relationship is governed by the rules of social reality. As we get to know them, the relationship begins to develop its own rules. Our behavior and how we communicate is determined by the nature of the relationship. As our relationship progresses we develop specialized rules that are more applicable to the nature of the relationship.

Conversely, the more impersonal the relationship, the more likely we are to continue to follow set patterns of communicating determined by social reality. For example, we often greet people by asking, "How are you?" The standard reply is to say that we are fine. When we get to know someone better, we might tell them how we really feel.

We develop rules in relationships based upon our past experiences. It is not uncommon for us to try to replicate what we perceive as a past success while avoiding past mistakes or repeating a bad experience.

The social aspects of a relationship are important because nobody wants to work all the time, we want to enjoy things as well. Relationships help us to fulfill important social needs, reduce tension, and to share interests with others.

In business situations where the focus is on getting tasks done, having social time is essential to healthy working relationships. People need to have time to get to know one another, to relieve stress, or just have fun. This is one reason why co-workers socialize by going to lunch or out together after work.

Relational Development

All relationships have one thing in common, at one time the people involved did not know each other. This means that all relationships go through the process of relational development. This process can be characterized by four phases that are governed by the laws of uncertainty, shared meaning, and investing. How a relationship goes through these phases depends on the nature of the relationship, the individuals involved, and their desired outcomes.

I. Relational Creation, The Law Of Uncertainty Phase.

When we first meet someone we are unsure of how to communicate with them. So, we rely on familiar patterns of communicating governed by the rules of social reality. We use the perception process to obtain information about them in order to help us know how to proceed. Based on the information we have, we try different approaches looking for one that will work.

There is often an awkward tension or stiffness when we first meet someone, because we feel self-conscious, perhaps even uncomfortable not knowing what to do or expect from them. Before we can form a relationship, uncertainty needs to be reduced.

The first phase of relational development is motivated by the law of uncertainty. The first time people get together is generally based upon the connections they have with one another. They may communicate with one another because they are in close proximity, have similarities, communicate frequently, or share common interests. They may seek to form relationships in order to fulfill needs and wants they cannot fulfill themselves.

Whenever we encounter a new situation that we are unfamiliar with, we look for ways to communicate with others. If we had to figure out how to communicate in each and every situation it would take too much time and energy.

So, as part of the rules of social reality people have developed patterns of communicating that tell us how to communicate and behave in various situations. These are pre-established ways we communicate with others that work rather like a script works in a play or movie. We use them because everyone knows the lines and what to expect, which reduces uncertainty.

We often use these patterns in unfamiliar situations like a job interview, moving to a new neighborhood, going to the grocery store, or visiting an unfamiliar place. Some patterns are simple greetings and others are more complex ways of interacting. They are commonly used because they meet our shared expectations, which reduces uncertainty making people feel more comfortable.

When we hear the same words repeated it gives us feelings of comfort and familiarity. When familiar patterns are not followed, it can increase uncertainty, which is why people might feel uncomfortable if they are changed too much. In many situations the expectations of others will determine what we say and do.

In new or unfamiliar situations it can be helpful to be aware of what others are doing. Let them go first and follow their lead. Be honest about your knowledge of the situation. If they know that you are new to the situation, they should be sympathetic to your circumstances and be willing to help you.

Asking others for their help or advice is a good way to start. If they do not know you, they may have unrealistic expectations of you and your behavior. If you show an interest in them, they are more likely to be receptive to you.

Forming relationships.

Think about the people you know. How did you get to know them? Do you remember the first time you met?

In relationships there is a connection that forms the basis of how we get to know someone. We cannot form a relationship with someone without first making a connection.

The most common ways we meet people are those who we see on a regular basis through everyday activities such as work, school, church, in our community, or doing errands. The closer their proximity, the greater the frequency, and the more intense the connection, the greater the likelihood of developing a relationship.

In order to develop a relationship, we must first meet someone we do not know. Because there is a higher degree of uncertainty, when we first meet someone we can feel uptight or apprehensive. We can be overly self-aware or self-conscious because we want things to go well.

Whenever we meet someone we can feel a high degree of uncertainty. We may feel apprehensive because we don't know what to expect from them or how they will behave. So, we might put up an invisible barrier for self defense to keep others out. However, this could increase uncertainty by making them feel threatened.

When we decide we want to meet someone we need to get their attention. We can't meet them without making a connection. A good way to make connections is through someone you already know. If you can have someone you know introduce you to them it reduces uncertainty and takes the pressure off you.

If having someone else introduce you is not feasible, you might find a reason to talk to them. Asking an open-ended question is a good way to start because it gets the to talk. It could be asking them if they know someone you know, asking what time it is, or for directions.

It is helpful to look friendly and open to conversation. We like to meet people who seem confident, relaxed, open, and approachable because it reduces uncertainty about them.

First impressions can be difficult to change even though we may not actually re-member the first thing someone said to us. This is because first impressions are not only about what you say, but how you say it and how others perceive it. Impres-sions are based on perception and much of what we perceive comes from nonver-bal communicating through body language.

Creating a good first impression comes from acting confident, self assured, and friendly. If we are perceived as being relaxed and at ease it makes us appear less threatening, so other people are more likely to be at ease with us.

Appearance as communicating.

Appearance is about how we look, our attractiveness, how we do our hair, the clothes we wear, and what all those things communicate to others.

Ideally, our appearance shouldn't matter. What should matter is who we are on the inside as a person. However, our appearance does matter because of the law of uncertainty. A person's appearance can be the most information we have about someone, especially if we don't know them very well.

Society invests personal appearance with meaning. People judge others by their appearance because it can be perceived as an outward manifestation of their inner qualities. Since people cannot see who we are on the inside, they look for information from our appearance.

They perceive our appearance and compare it to their expectations based on other people they know. They do this in order to make inferences about what a person is like without having to get to know them.

The law of uncertainty motivates us to gravitate toward people who we perceive are like us because they seem familiar. The rationale is if they seem similar to us, they must be like us and we will have something in common with them.

This is why people often associate with others who they perceive are like them and share similar characteristics like their age, culture, ethnicity, profession, or geographic affiliation. It's not necessarily a matter of discrimination, it's a means of uncertainty reduction.

We invest many characteristics of a person's appearance with meaning including their clothing, accessories, and hairstyle. This is because appearance can communicate a person's personal preferences and professional affiliations.

For example, a dark suit conveys a different meaning than a T-shirt and jeans, a uniform, or overalls. We attribute meaning based upon the perception process where we take information and give it meaning, then compare it to other people from our past experiences. Appearance can convey a variety of meanings about a person's attitudes, values, preferences, education, profession, ethnicity, culture, and personal preferences.

In order to work with others, we need to reduce uncertainty enough so that we feel comfortable with them. We are more likely to reduce uncertainty when our appearance is familiar to us or similar to our own, so we feel more comfortable about them.

Our appearance can work like our Great Idea in the process of communicating. It communicates information through connections to others who provide us with feedback about how they perceive us. If they like us, it has a positive effect on our self-concept.

Appearance provides the first bits of information others perceive about us to form a first impression. We use our perceptions to make decisions such as if we want to talk to someone and how to approach them. Even before we speak to them we develop expectations based on our past experiences.

Identity Management

When you introduce yourself to someone you have never met before, what do you say? What information do you include and what do you leave out? What do you say first, second, or last? Do you talk about your work, family, past experiences, or interests? Do you introduce yourself the same way in every situation?

How we introduce ourselves is influenced by the rules of social reality, our inferences about the expectations of the situation, and the people we meet. How we do this is the process of identity management.

Next time you meet someone for the first time, afterwards try to remember what you say about yourself. This can help provide insight into how we perceive ourselves and our expectations about how we would like others to perceive us.

Identity management is about the choices we make about what we say and how we behave when we communicate with others. This works like public relations, we make choices about what information we communicate to others that can shape their impression of us and to help us achieve our desired outcomes.

When we meet other people, we communicate information about ourselves whether we choose to or not. We may choose what to say, but we cannot choose to stop communicating nonverbally.

How others perceive us, as well is how we perceive ourselves, is partially based upon our individual characteristics. Others use these characteristics to gather information about us to make inferences about who we are to reduce uncertainty about us.

We manage several identities because we present ourselves in different ways in different situations. This can be based on the roles we fulfill, the context or situation, the groups we belong to, and our desired outcomes or the needs and wants we are looking to have fulfilled.

In each of the situations, we present a different identity based upon the expectations of others. This means that we could have a family identity, a work identity, and a public identity.

Each of these represents a part of ourselves that we present to others based upon the situation and expectations of the other people. For instance, we would not behave the same way at home as we might with our friends or at work or in church.

We do this to fit in with the expectations of others to reduce uncertainty, so that they will invest in relationships with us. People want to be around others who they perceive as being stable and predictable

We manage our identity by making choices about what information to share with others. Sometimes we manage our identity by choice, other times we don't think much about it so it happens naturally. We make these decisions based upon the situation, people's expectations, and the rules of social reality.

Conversation.

In order to create a relationship, we must first make a connection. One of the most common ways we do this is by engaging in conversation. This makes conversation one of our most important communicating skills. We have many conversations every day with our friends, family, or coworkers. We usually don't think much about these conversations because we have done this many times before and we know what to expect.

Whenever we meet someone we don't know, there is a natural uneasiness, awkwardness, or tension. This feeling comes from the high degree of uncertainty we feel when we don't know much about someone.

We can have a natural tendency to watch what we say and do because we do not know what to expect from them. However, we want to meet other people because it is enjoyable and we learn things by talking with them.

So, in order to communicate effectively with others and get to know them enough to develop a relationship, uncertainty must be reduced to create an atmosphere that is relaxed and comfortable enough to communicate with others. Developing conversational skills can help ease the tension and reduce uncertainty to create a more pleasurable experience.

We are motivated by the law of uncertainty to communicate with people to learn more about them. Getting to know someone through conversation is nonthreatening and a way to do this because it helps reduce uncertainty, which is necessary for any relationship.

The law of shared meaning motivates us to share information about ourselves, so we can get to know others better. The law of investing motivates us to communicate with others, so we can invest our resources in a relationship.

In practically all aspects of life, conversation is an important skill because it is how we meet and get to know others on a more meaningful level. Since relationships have both a task and social aspect, it is helpful that we can communicate not only about the task at hand, but also engage in social conversation.

We engage in conversation to develop connections that enable better working relationships. Most people do not make decisions simply on the task ability of an individual, they also consider their social characteristics. People want to work with others who not only can do their job, but who are enjoyable to work with as well.

In order to reduce apprehension and develop conversational skills, it can be helpful to practice talking to people you come in contact with while doing everyday tasks.

Talk about something that you like or is familiar to you. This should give you a natural self-confidence because you know something about what you are talking about. This will make you appear positive and upbeat because it's something you enjoy.

When you are confident and upbeat the other person should pick up on that and respond similarly. Not everyone will engage in conversation, so if they don't, don't take it as rejection.

When you first talk to someone, instead of opening with a line, get the conversation going by asking open ended questions. A person is more likely to answer a question because they want to be perceived as being helpful or polite. The question should not be overly complicated and be related to the context of the situation. If there's no response ask them again or ask another question.

The purpose is to get the other person to talk. Asking them what they think or how they feel about something shows that you are interested in them and encourages conversation. Anticipate questions others might ask you and have short, to the point answers ready. If you have to think about it for too long they may think you are not being honest or making it up.

Have a couple questions in mind to begin a conversation that can fit various situations. Don't over rehearse what you are going to say or use clever one liners because they can sound insincere.

Start with familiar topics of conversation. Be positive, keep the conversation light, and start with basic information. Talk about things you know something about and look for ones that you both are interested in to keep the conversation naturally going. Let the situation work for you by talking about something close at hand like what's going on around you.

At an appropriate moment in the conversation you might introduce yourself. When we introduce ourselves to other people, we often say things about ourselves like our name, what we do for a living, or a common interest.

Ask the other person their name and repeat it once out loud. Saying their name communicates that they matter and helps you to remember it. If you say it wrong they have the chance to correct you.

All too often we hear a person's name once when we first meet them and then forget it. After awhile we get to know them, but we can't remember their name and by then it's too embarrassing to ask them.

A good conversation is balanced, it has give and take. Avoid speaking too long without the other person saying anything. If you find you are talking too much ask the other person what they think to shift the balance. Think things through before you say them and give the other person time to respond.

Listen when they are talking. It is easy to only think about what to say next and not hear what others say. Actually listening to them should help you know what to say next by following up what they said. By listening and responding to what they say the conversation should begin to flow naturally.

Use positive nonverbal body language. Smile, nod your head, and gesture occasionally to indicate that you are interested and engaged in the conversation. Make appropriate eye contact.

Not looking at them can make you seem uninterested and staring can make people uncomfortable. Eye contact indicates that you are interested in them and are listening to what they have to say.

No conversation lasts forever, so have a way end it. It's better to wrap it up when it's going well rather than running out of things to talk about. Clearly signal the end of the conversation. How this is done depends upon your desired outcome.

To wrap up a conversation tell them that you need to go, to circulate, or see someone depending on the situation. Tell them that it was good talking to them. Since it is the last thing you say they are more likely to remember it than your opening because now they know you.

If you want to contact them again, say something like, "I have to go, but it would be nice to talk with you again." This gives them an opening to follow up if they are interested. It shows that you are looking to continue the conversation later on. However, don't say this unless you actually intend to do it.

II. Relational Growth, The Law of Shared Meaning Phase.

The second phase of relational development is motivated by the law of shared meaning. People need to share meaning in order to develop a relationship. When they are comfortable around each other, they begin to talk about themselves and share stories about their experiences.

Relationships are motivated by the law of shared meaning based on the connection between people. This motivates them to self-disclose so that they can better understand one another and communicate more effectively.

Since a relationship is a separate entity created by the people involved, each person has only partial control over it. So, it can develop its own unique personality that may be different from the people involved.

In order to create effective relationships, we need information about others to reduce uncertainty so that we can invest in relationships with them. Much of what we learn about other people can be rather superficial, which won't help us develop meaningful relationships.

Self-disclosure is the means by which we develop a relationship in ways that conversation cannot accomplish. It is the way we share meaning to reduce uncertainty, so that we can invest the time and resources necessary to develop a relationship.

We self-disclose in order to reduce uncertainty and share meaning about ourselves and others. When we know more about others it reduces uncertainty through sharing meaning, so that we can develop a relationship.

Self-disclosure helps us to improve our self-concept because when others self-disclose to us it can make us feel like we are valued. This can improve our confidence. It can be cathartic as a way to release tension by expressing our feelings and emotions. We feel better when we can confide in another person to share what is on our mind.

When we self-disclose it encourages other people to talk about themselves. We want others to reciprocate and when they do, we feel more comfortable with them. This reduces the level of uncertainty, so we feel more safe and secure around them.

Self-disclosure does not always go smooth. Others may be reluctant to share information about themselves. If others don't reciprocate, we can be less likely to continue and the relationship could stagnate or dissolve.

Most relationships never get beyond being a casual acquaintance. So, it's helpful to be realistic about our expectations of just what others want. The rules of social reality regulate how much information is appropriate to disclose in a particular type of relationship.

We are expected to share basic information about ourselves with others without going into great detail. As we get to know someone, we share more personal information about ourselves. Self-disclosure should be done in an appropriate way and at an appropriate time.

What we disclose can range from very basic types of information to personal thoughts and feelings. In any relationship disclosure starts out with very basic information and depending upon the nature of the relationship, progresses to consecutively deeper levels.

Impersonal self-disclosure is what we do in daily conversation. It involves small talk about topics that are of little significance like the weather, sports, current events, or the present situation. This is information that we have no problem sharing with others.

As we get to know someone uncertainty is reduced and they become more familiar, so we are more comfortable being around them. We may talk about our interests, likes, and dislikes. This helps us to get to know others on a more personal level.

You may have had the experience of meeting someone for the first time who tells you their entire life story. Rather than developing a relationship, you likely felt uncomfortable and just wanted to get away from them because it's an inappropriate degree of self-disclosure with too much information communicated too fast.

In business, self-disclosure needs to be done appropriately. This involves how suitable information is to share with others in a given situation. Personal information should be shared in an appropriate manner based upon the circumstances, the other person, and the nature of the relationship. Start with basic, publicly known information gradually moving to more personal information.

It is important to exercise good judgment about what we share because some information may be appropriate to disclose while some is not. In a new relationship start with conversation about things that are commonly known about you. Once you get to know somebody you can share more personal information.

Not everything constitutes self-disclosure. Talking about the weather, traffic, or current events is not necessarily self-disclosure. In some circumstances it may be perceived as way to avoid having a real conversation.

Where we self-disclosure depends upon the type of information shared. Generalized information can be shared just about any place it comes up in conversation. However, personal information should be shared in a more private location where there is no chance that someone could overhear it.

When we disclose information can make a difference in how it's received. The information you disclose should be relevant to what is happening at the time or reasonably soon afterwards. A good approach is to set aside a time for self-disclosure when things are not stressful and you can give it your full attention.

Self-disclosure works when one person shares information about themselves and then the other person shares similar information about themselves. Just because one person discloses information about themselves does not mean the other person will share the same information.

Start with a go slow approach because you can always add additional information, you can't erase information you have already disclosed. More information is not always better for disclosure.

Be aware of the other person's response to help you determine the appropriateness of the information you share. You always have the option of what information to share, when to share it, and with whom. Or whether to share it at all.

Self-disclosure can be difficult or uncomfortable, so it's helpful to show that you support others when they self-disclose. This is done by listening, providing feedback, responding appropriately, using positive gestures like eye contact and nodding your head to show that you understand what they are saying.

Not everything about us should be self-disclosed. Some things are better kept to ourselves, especially if they could damage the relationship.

III. Relational Maintenance, The Law of Investing Phase.

Relational maintenance can help to avoid potential problems. Relationships provide benefits, but they also require resources like our time and energy.

Our relational satisfaction is based upon our perceptions and expectations. People have a perception of their relationships that includes what they are willing to contribute based upon their expectations of future benefits.

The degree of relational maintenance depends on the type of relationship. Acquaintances require little maintenance. For the most part, all that's necessary is to be polite and friendly following the rules of social reality.

In professional relationships we may do things for customers or clients, send birthday or holiday cards to coworkers, or go out to lunch or dinner. More relational maintenance is necessary to maintain higher level relationships like with our friends and family. This is because we have higher expectations about them and have more invested.

As a relationship develops, needs and wants change. It can be helpful to be aware of these changes so that they can continue to be fulfilled. If not, a lack of awareness can make people dissatisfied undermining their commitment to the relationship.

If they are being reasonably met, then the relationship is being maintained. If they are not, then the relationship may be headed for difficulty. If detected early these situations can be remedied by talking about them and taking appropriate action.

IV. Relational Dissolution, Return To The Law of Uncertainty Phase.

It is said that all good things come to an end and so do our relationships. We spend time creating and maintaining relationships. So, when a relationship comes to an end it can make us feel sad, upset, even angry. The end of a relationship, especially a close one, can be very traumatic.

However, we spend little time considering how our relationships may come to an end. Forming relationships is a natural and inevitable part of life, and so is ending them. The reality is all relationships eventually come to an end.

Culture

Culture is a specialized version of social reality created by groups of people over time that helps to reduce uncertainty about themselves and the world around them. It is a means to make connections and share meaning through customs, traditions, and specialized ways of communicating.

Culture is usually associated with a specific geographic area and group of people. It influences many aspects of life including art, music, literature, food, clothing, religion, and architecture.

In business today we are likely to meet and work with people from many cultures. However, people from different cultures may find it difficult to communicate with one another because they perceive cultural differences as increasing uncertainty.

Understanding culture helps us to communicate more effectively by seeing things from other people's point of view.

When we meet someone for the first time we look to reduce uncertainty about them, so we might utilize information about culture based upon our past experiences to make inferences about them. Culture can potentially increase uncertainty when we meet others from a culture we know little about because we do not know what to expect.

People have many of the same needs and wants, but different cultures have different ways to fulfill them. Many of the ways that people fulfill their needs and wants are identified with culture. Learning about how different cultures approach things in different ways can help us look at the familiar in new and different ways.

Culture shapes how we perceive the world around us because it is the expression of a collective shared meaning. It provides perspective on how to interpret people's experiences. It can be a powerful force because it motivates people to take action and communicate based on what they perceive around them.

In order to reduce uncertainty we might make inferences about people based upon their culture from information we have gathered in the past. Even though this information may not be accurate, we do this in order to make them more familiar. This can lead to generalizations that could give us a false impression of someone before we get to know them.

Culture is an expression of social reality, so we may not be aware of how much it affects us. It is helpful to have an awareness of our own culture as well as how others differ. By being more aware of other cultures we gain a respect for them as well as an appreciation of our own.

Different cultures fulfill similar needs in different ways. These are some areas to be aware of where cultures can be different.

Cultures have rules regarding the use of personal space and what types of personal contact are considered appropriate. Some cultures value following the rules of etiquette where others are more casual and informal. Some hug or kiss on the cheek, while others shake hands, bow, or keep their distance.

Cultures celebrate traditions that include events from everyday activities, to annual holidays, to special events. The events that people celebrate are often based upon cultural traditions.

Cultures interpret how people use time differently. Some cultures value punctuality, when dinner starts at seven, it starts at seven and being late shows disrespect. Some cultures utilize approximate time, when dinner starts at seven it's okay to show up a bit late. Some cultures have more relative time, dinner starts when everyone gets there. It is helpful to be aware of how a culture views time, so you don't unintentionally upset people.

What is humorous is often based upon how language and common knowledge is utilized. Humor can be subjective. What may be funny in one culture may not be in another. Be careful using humor until you know people better.

Cultures have their own unique food and drink. These are often made from local ingredients and represent long standing traditions that are part of special events and celebrations. Guests are often treated to these specialties.

Cultures often have their own styles of artistic expression based upon their heritage and traditions. This can consist of unique styles of music including traditional and contemporary music.

Geographic affiliation.

Culture is often connected to specific geographic areas. Geographic affiliation refers to any place that we may feel a connection to like a neighborhood, community, city, state, region, or country. This could be where we were born, where we grew up, or where we live now.

A geographic affiliation can become a part of our self-concept and how we see ourselves. It reduces uncertainty because it can give others information about who we are based upon our geographic affiliation.

Cultural involvement.

When people become a member of a new organization or move to another country, they can be motivated by uncertainty to keep their own ways of doing things. They may seek out and spend time around others they perceive are like themselves. They may avoid people who already live there making them feel disconnected. Uncertainty can make them apprehensive to make connections with others and then they may wonder why they don't fit in.

Becoming involved in other cultures can help us to appreciate our own. Cultural diversity often emphasizes differences between cultures, which can be problematic when they rely on generalizations that may not be universally applicable.

Culture is not only associated with nationalities and geographic regions, it can also be a part of groups and organizations. Culture is a way of characterizing a group's social reality including its norms of behavior and how people communicate with one another.

External and Internal Culture.

External culture is the culture of the society in which a business exists. Internal culture is the culture of a specific business or organization. It is created by its members within the larger external culture. Because an organization may be located in different cultures or have members from several external cultures, they may have different styles of communicating and norms of behavior.

This can make it difficult for members to work together increasing uncertainty because they may feel unfamiliar with one another. This could reduce the effectiveness of an organization because people may not invest in relationships due to increased uncertainty.

By utilizing the law of shared meaning, members can develop an understanding of an organization's culture to reduce uncertainty, so members of different cultures know what to expect of one another making it easier for them to work together.

A business is immersed in an external culture, which affects its own culture. This can include local cultural traditions and rituals that can be part of the social activities of the organization. An organization can gain knowledge of the local culture by making connections to the local community and by participating in and promoting local community activities and events.

Uncertainty can be reduced by making connections between people of different cultures across the organization, so they know more about one another. Creating a positive social climate encourages them to communicate with one another, so that they can work more effectively together.

Organizations that have members from different cultures and specializations can work together more effectively by developing common communicating skills that reduce uncertainty.

When people know what to expect, it can increase their satisfaction and commitment to the organization. This helps develop a common culture so that people from different parts of the organization can work effectively together.

When brought together to accomplish a task, they can get to work on the task without having to figure everything out because they will know what to do.

It can be helpful to take a balanced approach to experiencing a new culture by maintaining familiar traditions, but following the local patterns of communicating, rules of behavior, and participating in local rituals and traditions. Getting involved in a culture can be the most effective way to learn about it and gain a greater understanding of others.

However, we may be reluctant to do this because we do not know what to do. Or we might read about a culture and then act as if we know what we are doing. Even the best information may be out of date or inaccurate. It is better to acknowledge not knowing about a culture rather than trying to act like you do.

Being straightforward about your understanding of a culture communicates that you are honest, open minded, and have an interest in it, so people should be open to telling you about their culture.

Diversity tends to be approached in terms of the differences that make us unique. Emphasizing differences can increase uncertainty. By thinking about culture in a new way, we can look for commonalities to make connections with others so uncertainty can be reduced.

The purpose of cultural understanding is not to create division, but create connections that bring us closer together by emphasizing the similarities that can create shared meanings with others.

This helps to reduce uncertainty about one another, so we can get to know each other better to form relationships. We can utilize the law of shared meaning to understand more about each other as well as ourselves. We can make connections to share meaning with others to understand them better to create common ground.

We invest in others to develop relationships with them. While we are culturally different, we are similar in that we seek to fulfill similar needs and wants, and achieve mutual desired outcomes.

People of all cultures join groups and organizations in order to fulfill needs and wants, form relationships, and achieve desired outcomes. These are things everyone has in common that can encourage them to make connections to help them understand each other.

Balancing Work and Family

Family is something we all have in common. We are born into a family, grow up in a family, and may form a family of our own.

It can be helpful to understand how families communicate because of the influence they have in our lives. Families affect our self-esteem, shape our perception and expectations, and influence our desired outcomes. They can create their own social reality that affects our thoughts and behavior.

Families form our closest, most personal relationships because we live with them, know them very well, see them often, and care about them. Families have the means to fulfill their member's needs and wants to create stability, security, and predictability.

We share meaning with our families to learn what it means to be a person and how to function in society. Families help us to develop important skills. It is in our family that we learn about ourselves, others, and the things around us. In families we share our ideas and experiences with others and they share theirs with us. We learn about things from their knowledge and experience.

Through the process of communicating, families shape our self-concept by providing us with reflected feedback. When we receive positive feedback, it bolsters our self-concept. When we receive negative feedback it can be harmful because it comes from people we are close to and whose opinion we care about.

We have expectations about our family and perceptions about how those expectations have been met. Tension and conflict can arise when our perceptions do not meet our expectations. In order to avoid this, it can be helpful for family members to communicate their perceptions of how those expectations are being met.

Family structure.

In order to function, families need structure to provide stability. Family structure consists of a family's roles, rules, and boundaries. Structure helps to organize a family to let everyone know who is responsible for what. Families have many types of structures, the most well known is a hierarchy often based upon age with grandparents at the top followed by parents and then children. This structure is often illustrated in a family tree.

Structure includes how families communicate, use time and space, and create boundaries. Family structures can range from strict to flexible. Flexible structures are easily changed or adapted, but can increase uncertainty. A stricter structure provides stability to keep things together by reducing uncertainty, but can be slow to adapt to changing circumstances.

Time is our most valuable resource and how a family uses it communicates what is valued by them. Children need structure, so they learn how to organize time until they are old enough to do it on their own.

If they do not have structure, they may not learn the importance of how to use time and may have difficulty as an adult. Having a regular schedule teaches children responsibility and helps to fulfill their need for stability.

Time structure involves how we schedule activities like when to get up in the morning, have meals, and go to bed. It is also how we schedule dates throughout the year like for birthdays and holidays. It gives the family stability and a sense of predictability by creating shared expectations of what the family will be doing together in the future.

How a family structures space includes not only how they use physical space, but also psychological space, like areas of responsibility and turf or territory. Our home has shared meaning representing safety and security because it is where we spend much of our time.

How we decorate it, the possessions we choose, and furniture we fill it with reflects our sense of style that expresses of who we are. We have many objects and possessions that have a story behind them, which invests them with meaning.

Families allocate space for individual members based upon their needs and status in the family. Who controls what space reflects the family power structure. Typically, the more powerful family members control more space.

For example, parents control most of the space in their home and perhaps have the largest bedroom. Children may have to share a space in a bedroom and have little say over how much of the family's space is used. As they get older they may want more control over their own space.

Family rules.

Rules are necessary to reduce uncertainty so that a family can function effectively. Rules govern our behavior, so everyone knows what is expected of them and they know what to expect from others. This creates structure, security, safety, and a degree of predictability. Having structure in families can make them a source of comfort and support.

Rules are important for children because they provide the structure and boundaries necessary for their development. If they do not learn how to utilize structure at an early age from their family, it may be more difficult for them to deal with structure when they become an adult.

Families have rules that everyone is expected to follow. Rules communicate and enforce the structure and boundaries necessary for their safety and security. However, some rules can go unspoken, so we don't know about them until we break them. The rules need to be clearly communicated to everyone so that they understand what is expected of them.

When they get older, parents can explain why the rules are important, so that the children will better understand why they are necessary. As they gain more responsibility, children can have a say in making the rules because by having a say in creating them, they are more likely to follow them.

Family roles.

Roles are shared expectations of individual behavior. Families have tasks that need to be accomplished, so somebody has to do them. Since everyone cannot do the same thing at the same time, they will take on different tasks creating roles. Members can have multiple roles like parent, child, sibling, or spouse.

Some roles, like parent and child don't change. Other roles, like who does the cooking changes depending upon a family's needs and wants. Having stable roles reduces uncertainty because everyone knows what they are supposed to do.

Family roles are based on the mutual perceptions and expectations of its members. When their expectations are similar and perceptions are realistic, they should feel that things are going well.

However, if there are different expectations of what each person is supposed to do or there's a perception that some people are doing more than others, it can be a source of tension or conflict.

Many roles are based upon a person's relationship with the rest of the family like parent, child, and sibling. They have responsibilities based upon their age and ability. The roles that have the most responsibility are typically done by adults and as the children get older they can take on roles with more responsibility.

Family tension.

A source of tension in families comes from different perceptions and expectations. Each person may expect to do things their way, so they are constantly struggling with each other. Tension may come from unfulfilled or competing needs and wants. It may come from the feeling of not being fairly acknowledged for their contributions.

The feeling that being a member of a family is hard work may indicate underlying problems from struggles over control, power, or allocation of resources. Developing clear norms, roles, and rules can help to relieve this tension.

Families can be one of our biggest sources of tension due to conflicting or un-fulfilled needs and wants. This is because we live in very close to other family members not only in close proximity, but also emotionally.

Family members can have conflicting needs and wants that can be a source of ten-sion. They need to spend time together, but they also need their own space. They need to feel a part of the family, but also have their own individual identity.

Having family members involved in making decisions shows that they are valued. They are more likely to support a decision if they are part of the process and un-derstand why it was made.

An effort should be made to resolve tension before it becomes a problem. It can help to be aware of each other's perceptions, expectations, needs, and wants. Fam-ilies need to talk on a regular basis. Some things may be difficult to talk about, but talking about them is better than letting them create tension, so being a member of a family won't feel like hard work.

In a family, if the parents are stressed or frustrated, they may have a diminished ability to help their children. If their relationship is weak or stressed they may not be as effective in their relationship with their children. If the parental relationship feels secure, then there's a much better chance that the parent child relationship will feel secure as well.

Parents should talk regularly with their children beginning at an early age because there may come a time when a child has problems and it will become necessary to have a talk with them. However, by this time things may have progressed to a point where dealing with it will be more difficult. The time to talk begins when children are very young.

It is easy to use the first style of communicating by only telling them what to do. Instead, try using the third style by engaging them in conversation, which encour-ages them to talk and give you feedback about what they are thinking and feeling.

Instead of the big talk, start with lots of small talks. Take your cues from your children, be honest, keep it simple, and keep the discussion age appropriate. Don't try to cover everything all in one talk.

Encourage them to think about things by asking open ended questions. There should be an ongoing series of conversations that parents have with their children over their whole life.

This can become a family norm. It begins an ongoing process of communicat-ing with your children so they trust you and feel comfortable talking about these things when they are very young and will feel comfortable talking to you when they get older.

Regularly communicating with your children not only provides information, it also reduces uncertainty about you, so they know that they can trust you and can come to you when they need something.

It helps to share meaning to make our experiences more significant to help you understand them better. It also makes them trust you more by investing in your relationship. When you know your children, you don't have to worry about what they are doing, because you know what they are doing.

Family commitment.

Families have a high degree of commitment. They help one another and are willing to sacrifice their own needs for the family and other members. They have a high degree of self-disclosure that reduces uncertainty creating feelings of being close.

Family commitment gives members the confidence to make sacrifices, work hard, and support their family without expecting anything in return. Because of the high level of investment, people often feel closest to their family members. But it can also be a source of tension and conflict.

Family members connect when they spend time together. They can share their thoughts and feelings or get help solving their problems. Doing this helps parents understand what their children are thinking and doing.

Families ask other members for advice to solve problems and to help them make decisions. This is how we show nurturing and support by creating closeness and commitment in relationships through the law of shared meaning. Doing this helps us build a positive self-concept making others feel valued and appreciated.

A family may wait until there's a problem before they talk with one another. They may even say, "We need to talk." Everyone knows this means that there is a problem. This can make communicating between family members stressful and negative because they wait until they have bad news.

In order to avoid having a talk as being a bad thing, families can have regular times where everyone gets together. A good time is over food. Families can have their own activities when everyone gets together. It can be a time to talk to one another without the pressure of having 'a talk.'

Families and food naturally go together.

Food is an important part of a family's traditions and rituals like when they celebrate holidays and other events. Preparing meals is part of what it means to be a family because it creates connections that bring them closer together. By cooking and baking children can learn about how food is made and why it's important.

It can be helpful for families to spend time together preparing meals because doing this can fulfill many important needs in addition to making something to eat. Doing this can help to reduce uncertainty by encouraging family members to talk to each other.

Preparing food encourages conversation. It can help them to share meaning because food is often connected to our past experiences, traditions, and heritage. It promotes investing in one another because they are spending time together.

Cooking and baking teaches children important life skills because everyone needs to know how to take care of themselves and their family. It teaches children how to follow a plan, how to budget, and how to choose and buy ingredients. It teaches them about food and where it comes from.

Everyone likes to eat, so cooking together can be a fun family activity. Then the family can sit down to share and enjoy what they made together.

Communicating with Food

Imagine what it would be like at a family gathering, work outing, conference, celebration, or special occasion without having anything to eat or drink. Think about what kinds of food and drink we share with others when we gather together for a birthday, wedding, holiday, or on a Sunday afternoon.

Communicating is about making connections between people and few things make connections better than food. We reduce uncertainty about ourselves by sharing food with others. We can learn about others by what foods they like. Holidays, celebrations, rituals, and traditions would not be the same without food.

Food brings people together, it helps us to develop relationships because we use it to meet people to make connections with them. When we want to build relationships with people, we may share a meal or go for coffee.

When we see other people, they often welcome us by offering us food as a sign of friendship. They may serve traditional food that represents their culture to make us feel welcome.

We use food to celebrate collective gatherings such as a convention where there may be a dinner or banquet. Food is used to celebrate important events in our lives such as birthdays, anniversaries, and weddings. Imagine what these occasions would be like without food and drink.

We use food to build business relationships. Coworkers may go out for lunch or have coffee breaks together. Sharing food encourages conversation, so people get to know one another better which builds relationships to help them work together. Food can be an great way to communicate because it utilizes multiple connections.

It can be colorful and looks good to us. We know many foods by their smell, which can be wonderful. Food has texture and some foods are eaten because of how they feel. Food can have sounds like when it has a crunch or sizzles while it's cooking.

Food tastes good to us giving us a feeling of contentment, fulfillment, and well being. Without any of these connections food would not be the same. Perhaps this is why food can be so satisfying, fulfilling, and even sensual, because it is one of the few things that makes a connection using all of our five senses.

Chapter 6
Creating Great Groups

What if you went on a job interview, but you didn't know what the job was for? What would you say?

What if you got the job and it was a really good job you didn't want to lose, but no one told you what you were supposed to do. What would you do?

After you were there for a while, you still don't know what to do. You don't ask anyone because you don't want to look like you don't know what you are doing and don't want to get fired. Now what would you do?

While this may sound unlikely, you may have experienced something like it without even knowing it. This is because when we join a group or organization it's likely that no one told you the unwritten rules that govern people's behavior in organizations.

Following the rules and norms of behavior can be more important to your success and job satisfaction than doing what you were hired to do.

Groups and organizations have rules that govern how people communicate and behave. The members may or may not tell you what these rules are, so you might break them and not even know it. Knowing how groups and organizations work can help you communicate more effectively increasing your chances of success.

Groups and uncertainty.

You have probably been a member of a group where things went well and you felt good about the group. You have probably also belonged to a group where things did not go well, so it felt like a waste of time.

This may have left you wondering what makes some groups more effective than others. Having knowledge of how groups work can affect how you feel about a group because having a good group takes effective communicating skills.

Forming and joining groups is a natural part of life. They are part of how we define ourselves as individuals. It is helpful to know how groups work because of the influence they have in our lives.

Groups can provide resources, affect our self-esteem, influence our perception and expectations, and affect our desired outcomes. They can create their own group social reality which gives them power over their members' behavior.

We are motivated to form groups and organizations to reduce uncertainty about ourselves, others, and the world around us. Groups reduce uncertainty by fulfilling many of our needs and wants. They create stability, security, and predictability. They have longevity beyond their individual members. The can acquire and allocate more resources than individuals.

Groups share meaning about the group and what it means to be a member. They share meaning through traditions and rituals creating their own customs and culture. Sharing meaning helps people to reduce uncertainty, so they are better able to invest in the group and the other members. Groups help their members to invest in one another and provide a means to protect those investments.

Members can feel comfortable investing in the group and the other members. Groups allow role specialization, so that each person can spend more time on specific parts of a task and learn skills they might not otherwise be able to do if working alone.

Groups contribute to our self-concept and affect how others see us. Groups help their members to reduce uncertainty about the group and the other members. They share meaning about the group and what it means to be a member.

Groups provide a means for members to invest in the group and in each other. They have a sense of collective identity. Members know that they belong to the group and each member considers themselves to be a part of the group. Members have a clear idea of what it means to be a member of the group and its traditions and history.

Groups have a network of connections between members through which they communicate that does not exist between people outside the group. Members often have a higher degree of interaction that creates an ongoing relationship.

There is a mutual purpose or desired outcome that the members of a group work together to achieve. In order to achieve their desired outcome, a group has tasks that members need to accomplish. Groups have a sense of collective outcome as they generally succeed or fail together.

Groups fulfill many of their members' needs and wants, which motivates them to join the group to have them fulfilled. Members work together to fulfill their own needs and wants, as well as those of the group. Groups allocate resources and make decisions, which gives the people who are in charge influence over others.

Groups have rules that govern individual and group behavior. Most often these are informal and communicated verbally. Larger more formal groups might write them down in a handbook or other document.

Groups have a process by which they get things done, make decisions, and resolve conflicts. Members understand and utilize this process in order to work together to achieve their desired outcomes.

Groups have many types of structures that can vary from formal to informal. They may have a hierarchy of how members relate to one another and who makes decisions. Groups have a shared sense of time and space. They spend time together as a group such as attending meetings or participating in activities.

Groups determine how members spend their time in the group. They often control physical space, like offices, and determine how that space is utilized. Members create their own psychological space, like territory or turf, by determining who is responsible for what.

Types of Groups.

• Purposely created groups. Many groups are formed intentionally to achieve a specific purpose or desired outcome. These groups are often have a structure to enable it to do more than individuals can accomplish alone. They tend to be task orientated like a business that produces a product or service. They can also be socially orientated, so people come together to share a common interest or hobby.

We purposely create groups in order to participate in activities and accomplish tasks with others in a way that fulfills our mutual needs and wants that it is beneficial for everyone.

• Newly formed groups. Every group has to be formed, so when a group first forms its members all join at the same time. This means that members are likely to be on an equal footing because there is no past history.

These groups experience a period of adjustment motivated by the law of uncertainty. This can be characterized by feelings of awkwardness where everyone is uncertain about what to expect from one another and from the group because they have no experience to give them the information they need.

If they know little about one another they will need to reduce this uncertainty through the process of self-disclosure, so that they can invest in each other to form the group.

Newly formed groups have to reduce uncertainty by determining many aspects of how the group works in order to function including their structure, roles, norms, and rules. Until this happens, they may have a difficult time working together.

• Existing groups. Most of the time we join an existing group where the other members already know one another and have a past history. They have already reduced uncertainty, shared meaning, and have invested in the group.

They may have already developed their group's structure, roles, norms, and rules. This puts a new member at a disadvantage because they know less about the group than the other members.

Even though the group is established, the introduction of a new member can put the group through a period of adjustment because they need to reduce uncertainty about the new member.

A new member must get to know the existing members and how things are done in the group. The new member will probably have little say at first about how the group works, so they need to conform to the group norms and rules.

• Task groups. The most common purpose for forming a group is to accomplish tasks, because more people working together can accomplish more things faster and more effectively. Even social groups have tasks that need to be accomplished for the group to function effectively.

• Social groups. Some groups are formed to fulfill the social needs of its members. They are often more informal and casual. All groups have social needs because working all the time is no fun and does not make a group very attractive or satisfying for its members. Even if the purpose of a group is to accomplish tasks, it needs to find a balance.

• Teams as groups. Some groups are referred to as teams and their work called teamwork. A team is always a group, but a group is not necessarily a team. A team is often a specialized type of group formed with a clearly defined desired outcome.

Whether the purpose of a group is task or social, they have tasks that must be accomplished to function. This means that members give up some of their independence by allowing the group to make some decisions for them in order to gain benefits from the group.

By participating in social activities we get to know other group members through the process of self-disclosure that includes telling stories about ourselves and our experiences. We get to know each other by participating in traditions and rituals like celebrating important dates and events.

Every group has to find its own balance between fulfilling task and social needs, but both of these must be addressed for a group to be effective. Some time should be set aside for each because they both cannot be fulfilled simultaneously. This can create a natural tension between the task and social needs of a group.

Why we form groups.

Life can be chaotic and unpredictable. So, we are motivated to form groups in order to reduce uncertainty about ourselves and others. While this is an important function of groups, having some uncertainty can be good. Groups need some degree of uncertainty to function effectively. When groups reduce uncertainty too much, they might stop looking for new information and generating new ideas because they no longer feel that they have to do so.

Members participate in rituals and traditions that serve to share meaning about the group. These shared meanings combine to create a history of the group that is communicated with other group members. Members communicate what it means to belong to the group. Over time these stories can create a common culture. Society is comprised of many groups and together these create social reality.

Through the process of communicating, groups can have a significant affect on our self-concept by providing us with reflected feedback. We utilize this feedback through the process of communicating to see ourselves as others see us. When we receive positive feedback it can bolster our self-concept.

Sharing meaning can make us feel an important part of a group, we can feel valued and appreciated as an individual. When others accept us it bolsters our self-concept and increases our confidence. Groups can give us a feeling of contributing to others and making a difference.

As a member of a group, when we need information or help to make decisions or solve a problem, we do not have to figure everything out for ourselves. Instead, we can seek out the help and advice of other members who might have done this before to make us more proficient sooner than we could on our own.

Because of the law of shared meaning we can understand and learn about things from the knowledge and experience of others without necessarily having to do all the work ourselves. As a member of a group we can seek out advice from other members who have had similar experiences to find out what worked for them to help us determine what we should do.

Groups and organizations provide an important means of implementing the law of investing. In relationships, we invest in the other person on an individual basis, so if the relationship ends, so do the benefits. Groups and organizations provide a mechanism that allows us to invest in many other people at the same time, even people we do not know.

Groups provide social benefits to their members in ways that individuals cannot. They can provide verbal praise, reinforcement, acknowledgment, support, respect, status, and prestige. These social benefits can be a powerful force motivating people to contribute to the group.

Being valued and accepted by others validates who we are as an individual by making us feel appreciated bolstering our self-concept, which can help to fulfill our needs and wants like acceptance, affiliation, and support.

Groups can provide monetary and material benefits. We invest our time, energy, and other resources in the group and each other in order to fulfill mutual needs and wants. Investments are regulated by the group's rules and norms, which determine how resources are allocated to its members.

As a member of a group, we make connections with many people providing a means to invest in several relationships instead of getting to know only one person at a time.

We are motivated to do this because our contribution to the group may be little more than we would contribute to an individual relationship, however, because there are many people in the group we can potentially receive more help and benefits. This saves time by not having to get to know everyone individually like we do when we form relationships

We all have perceptions and expectations about ourselves and others. These include what we think we are expected to do for others and what we expect others to do for us. Groups necessitate mutual contributions to achieve common goals by putting the group's interests ahead of the individual.

We have expectations about our experiences in the groups we belong to and perceptions about how those expectations are being met. Tension and conflict can arise when our perceptions do not meet our expectations.

Since everyone is different, all members of a group contribute differently leading to the perception that some people are doing more work than others, which can lead to tension or conflict in the group.

In order to avoid misunderstandings, it can be helpful for group members to communicate their perceptions of how those expectations are being met, so that they understand them better.

When everyone has an understanding of what is expected of them and what they can expect from others, the group can avoid unnecessary dissatisfaction that can lead to tension and conflict. When we are part of a group we might assume that the other members think like we do, but the reality is they may not.

The bank.

We join and stay a member of groups because they allocate resources that fulfill many of our needs and wants. So, when we join a group it could be thought of like joining a cooperative or being approved for a loan by a bank.

When we join a group, we can benefit from the resources it has to offer, but first we have to be approved by the members. This motivates us to seek their approval by reducing uncertainty about ourselves, so that the bank will accept us as a member.

When uncertainty is reduced about us, it enables the other group members to feel comfortable sharing their resources to invest in us, like having a line of credit to draw on. If the bank does not approve of us, the other members could be less likely to share their resources because investment in us can be perceived as having too much uncertainty.

When you become a member of the bank you agree to follow its rules. This includes the patterns of communicating and rules for behavior that have been determined as acceptable for its members. When members follow the rules, uncertainty is reduced and they are perceived as more stable making others more confident investing in them and in the group.

By following the rules we show that we are willing to make a commitment to the group and are worthy of receiving its benefits. Rules help to keep the group together because without them it would break down into chaos. This exerts a form of control over its members so that they are more stable now and more predictable in the future.

If we do not follow the rules, we can be perceived as less stable and uncertainty is increased. The group may exert punishments for infractions of the rules to keep its members in line. The bank has to do this because if it doesn't, then there's no reason for anyone to follow the rules and it will fall apart.

If infractions continue, we may be shut out or asked to leave the group, so that we no longer benefit from the resources of the bank, in effect closing our line of credit. If we leave the bank by quitting the group, we are no longer bound by the rules. So, we may be perceived as more uncertain and will not continue to receive its benefits.

This is why people can be motivated to stay in groups that they are not happy with or that they do not agree with because they do not want to lose the benefits they receive from them.

When individual members of a group invest in the group and its members, they are also investing in themselves. This is because when they help the group and the other group members individually, it benefits the group, which in turn benefits them.

When the group does well and is successful it can help make the other members successful. People are motivated to help one another as part of a group because they have a shared destiny or desired outcome.

When the members of a bank do well, then the bank prospers. When the bank prospers, individual members are likely to do so as well. Conversely, if they are reluctant to help one another or invest in other members, the group may not receive the resources it needs which can undermine its success and its members.

Groups and their members often have connections to other groups and individuals. A group may have the added benefit of allowing its members access to the resources of other groups and organizations, and their members. If a member of one group is approved and in good standing, they may also benefit from the resources of another group. For instance, if the group is part of a larger organization, like a department of a company, resources may be available to all the departments within the organization.

When a person ceases to be a member of the bank, such as if they quit or are removed, they are no longer permitted the full benefits of the bank. If they were allowed to keep them, there would be no reason to join the bank or follow its rules in the first place.

Group needs.

Groups are attractive because they have the resources and ability to fulfill many of our needs and wants. Groups can accomplish more to fulfill mutual needs and wants by working together than individuals can by working alone. Groups are able to mobilize resources for their members. They provide for material needs like a salary. We can learn how to do things by benefiting from the expertise and experience of others.

When more people are involved in problem solving there's a greater wealth of knowledge, experience, and expertise. Groups have the potential to make better decisions, solve complex problems, and provide the resources needed to get things done.

Groups are able to convey many kinds of social benefits that fulfill its members' needs. Groups can fulfill our need for prestige, esteem, and status in ways that we cannot fulfill as individuals. Not all groups are the same, we invest groups with meaning depending upon what they do and who belongs to them. Different groups are perceived differently giving them different levels of status and prestige.

For instance, a professional sports team can have a higher status than an amateur team. When someone joins a group the status of the group is often transferred to the individual member. Alternatively, if a high status person joins the group, the status of that person can be conferred upon all members of the group.

When a sports team signs a high profile player it can raise the status of the team and the other members. Some people join groups because of the status or prestige conveyed by the group upon its members.

The process of transference can work for prestige, respect, and self-esteem. If a group is respected or members held in high esteem, their status can transfer to other members of the group. If a member of the group does well, they may be held in high esteem and respected by other members.

This process can also work in reverse, if the group develops a negative reputation it can transfer the lack of status or prestige to its members whether they have deserved it or not.

Groups give people the chance to contribute, to feel like they are making a difference, to do something worthwhile, and to develop their talents. Groups often have a hierarchy within the group where members have different ranks or levels of importance. This motivates members to work for the good of the group so that they can improve their status or rank within the group. The ability to meet its members' needs and wants makes some groups more attractive or powerful than others.

Just as we experience tension as individuals, groups can experience tensions from conflicting needs, wants, and desired outcomes. As individuals, we have tensions between our conflicting and competing needs and wants, such as the need for stability and excitement. Groups can also experience tension between conflicting needs like the need for structure and flexibility. Individual members can experience tension between one another based on their own needs and wants.

For instance, members need to spend time working within the group to accomplish group tasks, but they also need to spend time by themselves away from the group with friends and family. Members may be unaware of these tensions and think there is something wrong with them or the others, which can lead unnecessary conflict. In order to be part of an effective group it is helpful to be aware that these tensions exist to mitigate their effect.

Groups have more resources available to them to make better decisions, but this may not happen because they can get caught up in tensions between competing interests. Members need to make decisions as a group, however, they often make decisions as individuals. Groups often take longer to make decisions than individuals, which can create tension.

To avoid unnecessary tension, groups need to develop a process to solve problems and make decisions. It is helpful to determine the rules for this process and the desired outcome before starting the decision making process, so that it goes smooth and in a time effective manner.

No two people see things exactly the same, so members will have different ideas. This can be a source of strength when group members bring different points of view together. However, more people means more potential sources of disagreement and tension. This is why groups should develop a process to deal with conflicts before they occur, so they can be resolved when they do.

Effectively managed disagreements can be good for groups because it tests ideas, so that they can come up with a better solution. However, it can be bad if it prevents the group from reaching a decision that everyone can support.

We are not a member of just one group, we are a member of many groups that have different expectations. This can cause tension between the expectations of one group with the expectations of another. This can make people feel uncomfortable or make it difficult for them to feel a part of some groups, and they might not know why.

It can be helpful to be aware that while rules are important to keep the group together, they could also hinder it from being effective by keeping people from feeling comfortable.

By being aware of this, groups can develop rules and norms of behavior to keep the group functioning while allowing for individual expression to keep members happy.

Groups provide benefits to their members that often come at a cost. Like other relationships, we may keep a balance sheet listing the benefits and costs in the back of our mind based on our perceptions and expectations.

The difference between our perception of what we contribute compared to our expectations of what we receive in return can have an influence on the satisfaction we feel and our commitment to the group.

While there is a common notion that people maximize benefits and minimize costs, or buy low sell high, nobody wants to be in a group with someone who wants everything and does little in return. Instead, people are likely to seek fair rewards for fair contributions.

If we feel that we are making fair contributions and receiving fair benefits in return, we can feel a sense of satisfaction that will increase our commitment to the group. However, if we feel we are contributing more than our fair share and receiving less than others, we are likely to become dissatisfied reducing our commitment.

This could motivate us to look at other groups as a comparison to determine how well we are doing. We may even think about leaving and joining another group. If enough members feel this way it can undermine the effectiveness of the group creating tension and conflict, which might cause it to breakup.

The group can avoid unnecessary tensions by encouraging its members to communicate their perceptions and expectations, so that they can be more in line with reality. Balancing responsibilities and benefits can help group members feel that they are receiving fair returns for fair contributions.

When we join a group we give up a certain amount of our individual freedom by allowing the group to make some decisions for us. We do this because groups provide benefits and allocate resources including monetary, social, and status benefits. In exchange, we give up some of our time, energy, and individual freedom.

When we join a group, like when we get a job, we give up some of our freedom to do what the group wants us to do. We do this because we have the mutual expectation that other members of the group will do the same for us.

Members contribute their resources and give up some individual freedoms for the benefit of all members of the group. This gives the group power to control the behavior and interactions of its members within the group by establishing norms, rules, and patterns of communicating.

Groups can help alleviate potential tensions between individuals and the group by clearly communicating the group's expectations for behavior and allowing for some degree of individual differences within the rules of the group.

They can have group members come up with some of the rules because people are more likely to support rules when they have a say in making them. The group can encourage individuals to take the initiative and support their efforts when they support the desired outcomes of the group.

Time is perhaps our most limited resource and we contribute a lot of our time to groups. We often measure our investment in groups based upon the amount of time we spend in them. The more time we spend, the greater our investment and commitment.

Group members may have different ideas about how to best utilize the group's time because it takes time to meet, make decisions, and get things done. How members perceive the group is using time can be a source of tension particularly if they perceive others are wasting it. This can cause members to become impatient or unhappy with the group.

Groups can reduce tension by being aware of how they are using their members' time to make sure that it is as productive as possible. If members have the perception that the group is wasting their time, they may become dissatisfied reducing their commitment or they might even leave the group.

While we choose many of the groups we belong to, we cannot always choose who else belongs to these groups. This can create conflicts between individual personalities creating tension. In some groups, members get along while in other groups they can be at odds with one another. Some members of a group may try to dominate or control the group for their own gain, while other members may hold back or withdraw.

While the group is made up of individuals, the focus should be on accomplishing group tasks. If the group is not accomplishing its tasks, members may become unhappy and not contribute to the group making it less effective. In order to reduce tension between members it's helpful to develop behavioral norms, methods of decision making, clearly defined roles, and other structural mechanisms that can help the group to achieve its desired outcomes.

These mechanisms help to keep overbearing members at bay and encourage those who may hold back to contribute. A group can balance these things by creating expectations that individuals will work cooperatively for the good of the group.

Groups have a shared sense of responsibility and each group member should assume responsibility for their actions within the group. Differences in individual perceptions and expectations may lead to tension or conflict over who is responsible for what tasks. Members may seek to avoid taking responsibility by claiming something was not up to them or that others were responsible for what happened.

In order to avoid this, clearly communicate who is responsible for doing what tasks and have a contingency plan if things do not go as expected. While one person may cause a problem, the other members may bear the consequences for what another member does, even if they had nothing to do with it.

Group members often have differing expectations about what kinds of changes are acceptable and which ones are not. Some people join a group hoping it will never change and some people join a group to change it. This can create tension between those trying to change the group and others who resist change.

This tension can waste the group's time and resources. In order for any changes to be successful, they have to be acceptable to everyone. Members need to be comfortable with change or they may work against it to undermine it. The more people feel something is at stake or that the change will cause them to lose something they have invested, the more they may work against it to try to stop it.

So, it's helpful to communicate the benefits of change and to have a process where everyone can contribute. When people have something to gain and they have a say in making the decisions that affect them, they are more likely to support them and see that they are successfully implemented.

We join groups in order to accomplish things that we cannot do as individuals. Ideally, our individual desired outcomes should be compatible with those of the group, however, this is not always the case. It is more common for a group's desired outcome to come into conflict with those of individual members.

There is a natural tendency for members to put their own needs, wants, and desired outcomes above those of the group. If the group is not meeting their needs and wants they are more likely to work for their own benefit rather than for the group.

This can be damaging to a group because if everyone pursued their own individual objectives, the group could not accomplish its tasks or achieve much of anything as a group.

In order for a group to function, the group's desired outcomes must take precedent over the individual's. This is because if everyone pursues their own individual desired outcomes there is no longer any purpose to having a group. However, if individual needs and wants are not fulfilled, tension is created and people might leave the group to have them fulfilled elsewhere. Putting group goals over your own creates interdependence between individuals because the outcome affects all of its members.

For example, a sports team either wins or loses. All members win or lose together collectively as a group. Because the outcome for all members is dependent upon one another, there is an incentive to work together. This creates interdependence where the desired outcomes of all the members are tied together. While not all groups have such a clear cut outcome, when a group is successful all members should benefit.

How groups are formed.

How do we meet people to form groups with or find groups to join? Sometimes it's by choice and other times it's by chance. Sometimes it's a bit of both. Groups are formed by making connections with others and communicating through those connections. In order to form groups we must first make a connection with others. To do this we have to meet them for the first time.

So, we often rely on familiar patterns of communicating that follow the rules of social reality. People create groups for reasons that can be as varied as the individuals who create them. We are motivated to create groups to help us fulfill mutual needs and wants that we cannot fulfill ourselves. The advantage of joining a group is that they can fulfill needs and wants on an ongoing basis rather than negotiating with others every time we need something.

In groups we get to know people over long periods of time reducing uncertainty increasing predictability and stability. Groups help us to communicate with others by making connections with them. Groups help make life more meaningful by sharing our experiences with others. Groups can provide structure and future predictability enabling us to invest resources in others to achieve desired outcomes. They increase security, stability, and predictability motivating us to form groups in practically all areas of our lives.

A group's identity is not so much about the individual members, but rather the relationships members create collectively with one another. This is why people can act one way in one group and a different way in another group. If members act as individuals, there is not much of a group identity. In order for them to be a group, there has to be connections and some degree of coordination between them. In order to do this, each person must give up something in order to gain something in return.

In relationships, two people communicate directly with one another negotiating everything between themselves creating a balance of power. Groups have a different climate because by adding a third person the balance of power shifts, changing the nature of how they communicate with one another.

Adding a third person can change the nature of how they communicate. Each person now divides their attention between the other two. Chances are each person spends more time with one person than the other creating an imbalance.

With three people there is the potential for two of them to make decisions giving them power over the third person. You have likely experienced a relationship with a friend who then got another friend, a girlfriend or boyfriend, or perhaps even got married. Chances are the nature of your relationship and how you communicated with them changed.

Groups usually have more than three people, but when we go from a two person relationship to three people or a larger group, how they communicate with one another changes. There will be people who communicate more with some and less with others. How resources are distributed can create an imbalance in the group.

In order to be part of a group, we have to make a connection with others so that we can meet them. Since we are only able to come in contact with a finite number of people, we have limited options of what groups we can join.

Group Development

All groups have one thing in common, at one time the group's members did not know each other. This means that all groups go through the process of group development. This process can be characterized by four phases that are governed by the laws of uncertainty, shared meaning, and investing. Since every group is different there is no best way to develop a group.

A group can go through these phases rather quickly or they might take some time. How a group goes through these phases depends on the nature of the group, the individuals involved, and the group's needs, wants, and desired outcomes.

Phases of group development.

1. Group creation, the law of uncertainty phase. Individuals come together to form a group motivated by individual needs and wants to achieve mutual desired outcomes. They may know little or nothing about one another, so they need to reduce uncertainty to function as a group.

2. Group growth, the law of shared meaning phase. Once uncertainty has been reduced to a level that members are comfortable with, they share meaning to develop their social reality, which includes the group's structure, boundaries, norms, roles, and rules of behavior.

3. Group maintenance, the law of investing phase. Once group members know more about the group, they begin to feel comfortable investing their time, energy, and other resources in the group and in one another in order to work together to achieve their desired outcomes.

4. Group dissolution, return to the law of uncertainty phase. There are times when a group no longer functions and may cease to exist.

I. Group Creation, The Law of Uncertainty Phase.

The first phase of group development is motivated by the law of uncertainty. People are first drawn together based upon the connections they have with one another.

People form groups for many of the same reasons they form relationships. They may be in close proximity, share common interests, or have similar desired outcomes. They are motivated to do this in order to reduce uncertainty, so that they can fulfill needs and wants they cannot fulfill as individuals.

Every group has one thing in common, at one time it did not exist. And every member has one thing in common, at one time they did not belong to the group. Every group had to be created and every group member has to go through the process of joining the group. Even if a person was part of forming a group, they still go through the process new members go through to get accustomed to the group.

When we meet with a group for the first time we want to make a good impression. We use identity management to shape the impressions others have of us by presenting ourselves as we want them to perceive us. We want to be perceived as likable, so they will like us because we like being liked.

We want to be perceived as agreeable, so they will get along with us. We want to be perceived as being helpful, so they will help us. We want to be supportive of others, so they will support us. We do this because we want to be perceived as someone who would be a good group member.

We want to make a good impression, so when we first get to know someone we reduce uncertainty by following the rules of social reality. We make a good impression by how we communicate, both verbally and nonverbally. We talk about general subjects to get things started while looking for specific topics that might be interesting to talk about.

We use conversational skills to create a natural flow being careful not to talk too much or too little. We utilize positive nonverbal body language such as smiling, facial expressions, and eye contact to make a connection.

In order to reduce uncertainty, we utilize information that is available to us when we first meet someone to develop a first impression. Since we don't know the others we probably have little information about them, so we form an impression based on the information that's available, such as what they say and how they use nonverbal body language. If there is information missing, we fill in the gaps using our past experiences, whether it is accurate or not.

When meeting new people we often have a heightened sense of self-awareness giving us a feeling of apprehension or anxiety. Anxiety is an emotional feeling based upon increased uncertainty. We might focus on how we are coming across to others because we want to make a good impression so they will like us.

This may create feelings of uncertainty or awkwardness in the conversation because we are searching for common ground as well as trying to determine how others perceive us. We don't usually consider that the others may also be just as concerned about how they are coming across to us. When we feel anxiety we are more likely to communicate on a superficial level.

This level of communicating cannot continue for very long because if there is too much uncertainty, people will not be able to get things done. This means that one of the first tasks a group faces is the challenge of reducing uncertainty, so that they can function as a group.

This can be done through conversation with appropriate self-disclosure, so that members can find common ground to reduce uncertainty enough to begin to function as a group. When they feel more comfortable with one another, they are better able to communicate in more depth and build common connections enabling them to get to know one another better.

Whenever we join a group we can find ourselves in an unfamiliar situation motivating us to look for ways to communicate with others. If we are not sure what to do, we may fall back on past experience, which may or may not help. If uncertainty is too high, we may hold back and not talk very much letting others do all the talking, which can make us feel like an outsider.

In these circumstances it can be helpful to use familiar patterns of communicating that are part of the rules of social reality. Patterns of communicating are pre-established methods of interacting with others that work like a script in a play or movie. They help to reduce uncertainty because we have heard them before. We use them because learning how to communicate in every situation we face would be difficult and time consuming.

We use patterns of communicating to reduce uncertainty in many common situations such as a job interview, first date, going to the grocery store, or meeting people we don't know. These patterns include simple greetings as well as more complex ways of interacting. They tell us what we should say and do to act properly in a given situation.

For example, a common pattern of communicating when we meet someone is to say, "Hello, how are you?" And the expected reply is, "Fine, thank you." We are not supposed to actually tell them how we feel. If we did, it would be unexpected and not part of the established patterns of communicating, so they may not know how to respond.

We use familiar patterns of communicating when we first form a group to get things going until the group members get to know each other well enough to develop their own ways of communicating. They may rely on their past experiences in other groups and behave in ways that they have done in the past.

This can create a feeling of stiffness and awkwardness within the group because everyone is uncertain how to communicate with one another. Some people may hold back by not participating letting others dominate the conversation.

While patterns of communicating work initially, a group cannot effectively accomplish its tasks or achieve its desired outcome in this manner. The group needs to develop its own method of communicating between members. By knowing how this process works, you can help your group to become more effective.

Balancing the group.

A group is only as effective as the individuals that comprise it. This makes the choice of who is in a group important to its success. Some groups develop naturally and members have little or no choice over who is in the group. Some groups are open to anyone who wants to join. Some groups are purposely created to achieve specific desired outcomes, so there may be criteria that determines who can join.

Choosing group members may be the single most important task facing any group. To create a group that works well together takes balance. Balancing a group involves balancing the roles people play within the group. It is finding the right combination of experience, skills, and expertise relevant to the task.

For example, a group made up of all leaders may have a more difficult time working together in a group than one that is more balanced with people who have experience in more supportive roles.

In choosing members for a group consider what they bring to the group. While it is important to give consideration to their expertise and work skills, they also bring with them their communicating skills, behavior, attitudes, and past experiences.

Consideration should be given to their social skills and ability to work with others. People may be good at what they do, but they might have difficulty working in a group with others.

Just as everyone has their own style of communicating, everyone has their own style when it comes to participating in a group. In selecting group members, consider how the group handles decision making, problem solving, disagreements, tension, and conflict. Group members should be willing to work for the good of the group by putting their own personal desired outcomes after those of the group. They should be able to plan, prioritize, organize tasks, schedule time, and contribute to the work of the group.

In selecting group members, consider each person's communicating skills, their participation in other groups, the roles they fulfilled, their commitment to those groups, and how well they work with others. It is helpful for members to have a connection so that they feel comfortable with one another to reduce uncertainty.

This will help them to work better together to accomplish their tasks. In addition to their ability to accomplish the task, members should have effective communicating skills because it will have a direct effect on the success of the group. It does little good to bring together a group of the best experts if they cannot communicate or work effectively together.

Since people join groups for a reason, consider their reasons for joining the group including their needs and wants, perceptions and expectations about the group, and desired outcome for themselves and the group. Everyone joins the group because they have their own needs and wants to fulfill. If they go unfulfilled, it can undermine their commitment to the group.

Group size.

In balancing a group, consider the optimum size to achieve the group's desired outcomes. A group needs to be big enough to accomplish its task, but not too big to detract from it. Size depends on the resources that will be needed, the task to be accomplished, and the individual member's abilities.

A workable size allows every group member to communicate directly with every other member. Groups are considered to be three or more people, but a more practical size can be from five to around twenty members. If a group is going to make decisions that involve voting it must have an odd number of people to prevent tie votes.

Group size has tradeoffs as there are advantages and disadvantages to both small and large groups. It's helpful to be aware of these in order to choose the optimal size for your group. Larger groups have more resources, information, experience, and expertise, but this does not mean that they make better decisions than smaller groups. They can handle more work by breaking a task down into smaller tasks and assign them to individual members to get them done more efficiently.

New members.

When a new member joins an existing group the current members might expect that nothing will change. However, a new member can increase uncertainty creating feelings of awkwardness. This is because the new person is uncertain what to expect from the group members and the existing members are uncertain what to expect from the new member. They will have to go through the process of self-disclosure and behavioral reinforcement in order to reduce uncertainty, so that they can work more effectively with one another.

The new member brings with them their past experiences from other groups, so they may expect to do things the way they did before. Even if their role in the new group is assigned such as in a job description, they will need to negotiate their own place within the group through the process of behavioral reinforcement.

When a member leaves the group and no one replaces them, the other members will have to pick up the slack and take over their responsibilities. If a new member is brought into the group to fill the vacant position, they will have to go through the process of behavioral reinforcement. This is how a new member can upset an effective group, by increasing uncertainty so it does not function as well.

By understanding and supporting the behavioral reinforcement process that groups go through, bringing new members into a group can be a much smoother and more positive experience.

Once a group has been established it may develop procedures to bring in new members. Some groups have restrictive guidelines for approving new members, while others are happy to have anyone join. Some groups allow new members to simply show up if they want to join the group, which means that they may have little or no control over who is a member. Other groups have a choice of who they recruit and criteria for accepting new members.

Choosing new members involves the same considerations as in balancing a group. Consideration should be given to a person's experience, education, expertise, and ability to accomplish the task. Consideration should also be given to their group skills such as their ability to work in a group with others, their commitment to the group, how they make decisions, and how they deal with tension and conflict. These skills are important because they determine how well they will work with others in the group.

No group remains the same, members leave and new ones join. So, it's helpful for groups to develop a mechanism by which new members can smoothly join the group and current members leave.

Groups can utilize the laws of uncertainty, shared meaning, and investing to help new members make a smooth transition into the group because they will need to renegotiate roles, norms, and rules to include new members. In formal groups, such as a business, new members may go through an orientation or training program to learn about the group or organization. Even in groups where there are formalized rules that are written down, there are often unwritten rules that a new member needs to learn.

A new member should be given time to get to know the other group members by encouraging self-disclosure to help develop relationships. New members can be more easily brought in to the group when they have time to socialize with existing members, so that they can get to know each other on a more personal level.

This helps fulfill task as well as social needs of the group and its members. Group members can go through the process of self-disclosure with the new member by taking time to talk about themselves.

Newcomers to an existing group can be at a disadvantage because they do not have the same knowledge about the group that existing members have. So, it can be helpful to learn about a group's history, rules, norms, and ways of communicating before joining it.

It can help to listen to stories members share about their past experiences and the group's history because they can communicate the values of the group. A new member can offer to do little things to help other members because it demonstrates a commitment to the group. They can learn the rules and norms of behavior including verbal, nonverbal, and body language, as well as how they use time and space such as decorating their offices.

Characteristics of an effective group member.

Be there, show up for meetings, be on time, and stay until the end. The most frequent complaint people have about other group members is that they arrive late, leave early, or just don't show up. This behavior can be perceived as a lack of respect for others that wastes their time.

Groups are about sharing resources in order to get things done. If you want to get something, you usually have to give something in return. Every group has tasks that need to be accomplished, so you need to contribute time, energy, expertise, experience, attention, or material resources to benefit the group.

Be courteous to other group members and show them respect in order to receive it in return. This creates a positive environment so that the group can work well together. It's important to do this whether or not the other members deserve it because being courteous is not about how they behave, it's about who you are as a person.

Do your homework and be prepared for meetings and activities. Not being prepared undermines the effectiveness of the group and wastes time for the group members who are prepared.

Groups need to get things done and effective groups share tasks fairly between group members. Group members are willing to pick up the slack when necessary. Know what is expected of you and fulfill those responsibilities because people don't like having to do the work of other members.

All groups have rules. Get to know what they are and follow them because without rules, the group could not function effectively.

One of the purposes of forming a group is to provide mutual support for one another that cannot be achieved as individuals. In a group you support the other members because you want them to support you. If they don't support you, look for another group that will.

Acknowledge the contributions of other members. Respond positively to their ideas and agree with them when possible. Support the group process to make and implement decisions.

Be fair, objective, and open minded. Consider what others have to say. Consider new ideas and new information. Consider the possibility that you might not always be right about everything all the time.

Avoid being overly critical of others, do not play politics, do not have hidden agendas, and do not act in your own self-interest. The group exists for the good of everyone not just to benefit one person or a select few.

Help the group achieve its desired outcomes. You can do this by putting group goals above your own personal goals. You can keep the group moving forward to accomplish its task by contributing, by evaluating information on its merits, and encouraging the group to make good decisions that will benefit everyone.

Help other members fulfill their needs and wants. By helping others, hopefully they will help you in return. If you help them and they don't help you in return, you might find another group that will.

II. Group Growth, The Law of Shared Meaning Phase.

When a group first comes together there is a high degree of uncertainty because people are unsure what to say and how to act creating an atmosphere of awkwardness and formality. Once group members get to know one another, they reduce uncertainty to a level that enables them to work together.

When members are comfortable with one another, they begin to talk about themselves and their past experiences. They share stories about themselves, others, and the group. This begins the law of shared meaning phase of group development. Sharing meaning helps to create a common understanding within the group of what the group means and what it means to be a member.

A group has meaning to both its members and those outside the group. A group can be like a person, it can develop a unique identity separate from the individuals that comprise it. Members may express that identity by giving their group a name and symbols like a logo, mascot, or group colors. If the group has been given a name by outsiders, like in a company or department, the members may put their own mark on it by giving it a nickname.

Shared meaning lets group members know what the group stands for and what it means to be a member. This is often communicated through the stories members tell and the group's history, traditions, and rituals. Groups can utilize identity management, much as individuals do, to manage what they communicate about themselves with people outside the group.

Groups, like individuals, have needs and wants that must be fulfilled to achieve their desired outcomes so the group can function. This motivates individual members to take action to accomplish them. Groups have many members to accomplish these tasks, but everyone cannot do the same thing at the same time.

This means that group members need to specialize by taking on specific tasks, roles, and responsibilities. Since there are many people doing many tasks, groups need structure in order to coordinate their activities. If everyone did whatever they wanted, the group would become chaotic and nothing would get done.

Developing a group structure includes creating rules and standard operating procedures which members accept as their normal means of behavior, commonly called norms. In naturally occurring groups norms are often not predetermined, so the members will have to create them as they go.

In groups that are intentionally created, like in a business, the structure may be established in advance, but the members may still need to negotiate how they will get things done. Behavioral reinforcement is the mechanism by which groups develop and solidify their structures like norms so that they can function effectively.

Self-disclosure.

Self-disclosure encourages investing in groups much like it does in relationships. It is a means by which we make connections with one another. When group members talk about themselves and their past experiences, they contribute to the collective experience of the group.

Disclosure begins at a very superficial level by talking about commonly known information such as where people live, what they do for a living, and their experiences. As people share information they become more comfortable sharing more personal information. As group members get to know one another it reduces uncertainty so that they are more familiar and predictable enabling them to trust each other to contribute their resources to work together.

Self-disclosure is more effective when done in incremental amounts over time, sharing only information that is appropriate to the group. Disclosure should be reciprocated so everyone feels like they are fairly contributing. This way no one feels they are contributing more information about themselves than anyone else.

We share information as we feel comfortable and when we feel it's appropriate. Too much disclosure, shared too fast can be considered inappropriate potentially scaring people away. Too little disclosure can be perceived as holding back, being evasive, or being aloof. Members can utilize feedback to determine the appropriate level of self-disclosure that itself may become a group norm.

Behavioral reinforcement.

Have you ever felt like you acted in one way when you were with one person and in a different way when you were with someone else? We can change our behavior depending upon who we are with because of the effect that they have on us.

Since a group is created by the people involved, it can develop its own unique personality. This is because we manage our identity based upon our perceptions of how others are perceiving us and our expectations in the relationship.

This happens because we have variable and non-variable characteristics. Non-variable characteristics include the things we cannot change about ourselves like gender or age. These are the things about us that do not change when our circumstances change.

Variable characteristics include those things about us that we can change depending upon our circumstances. They can include things such as how outgoing we are, our sense of humor, or what we like to talk about. Variable behavior is important because it allows us to act differently when we are out with friends, at work, or in church.

Our behavior changes depending upon the people around us. How we communicate depends upon the nature of the relationship. What is acceptable in one relationship may not be in another.

We behave differently in different groups because we are affected by the people involved in them. Every group has its own unique qualities that give it a distinctive character or personality. This means that it is possible for a group to become something that we do not want or do not intend it to be. This is why we may feel that a group is not going the way we want or that we don't have a say in it.

How this works can be illustrated by imagining two musicians playing on the same street corner. If each of them are playing their own song it would be difficult to hear either one of them and it would probably sound awful.

If they play the same song together it will sound much better. However, neither one has complete control over what the people passing by hear. They hear a combination of the two that neither can create by themselves.

When people in groups behave as individuals, like the musicians playing two different songs, it can become hard work that can increase uncertainty. When people are aware of how groups work they can work together to make the group less stressful, less work, and more beneficial to everyone.

When we receive feedback, other people have an affect on our variable characteristics, which can change our behavior. Different people have the potential to bring out different parts of our personality. This is why we may act one way in one group and in an entirely different way in another. We may even act in ways we do not expect.

Since a group is a separate entity with its own unique characteristics it can develop its own rules, structure, and norms of behavior, which may be the same or different than we have in our other groups. We may find ourselves with one set of behavioral norms in one group and a different set in another, motivating us to have different behaviors and communicate in different ways.

We manage our identity in our groups, and in each one we make different choices how to do that. Since a group is a combination of the people who created it, even though it involves us, we might feel like we have little control over it and may be surprised by the direction it is going.

Groups develop their own specialized ways of communicating and doing things through the process of behavioral reinforcement. This process begins by using familiar patterns of communicating as members exhibit behaviors to accomplish tasks based upon their past experience and perceptions.

The group selects which behaviors it deems appropriate for the group and discourages those it does not. To do this, members may utilize the process of communicating to share their Great Idea with others in the group and then wait for feedback. The nature of the feedback they receive at this early stage can determine the future behavior of the group.

Members communicate in different ways and exhibit different behaviors based upon their past experiences in order to find ones that work for them and the group.

This behavior is either accepted, rejected, or met with indifference by the other members. When a group member does something that the others approve of, they are encouraged to repeat it and if it's repeated over time, it can become part of the group's behavioral norms.

Agreement is a powerful social reward because it affirms our ideas, bolsters our self-concept, and improves our confidence. Once group behaviors have stabilized, they may be difficult to change. By being aware of this process you and the other members can utilize positive reinforcement to reward useful behavior to help the group become more effective.

Negative behavioral reinforcement discourages behaviors through the process of communicating. If we receive negative feedback it can hurt our self-concept motivating us to not repeat the behavior. If a member's behavior is met with consistent negative reinforcement it is not likely to be accepted by the group and should not become part of the group's norms of behavior.

If the feedback is unclear, the behavior will likely be repeated until clear feedback is received. If there is no feedback, it can be difficult to know what to do. If group members feel they are being ignored they may become frustrated and act out more forcefully leading to tension or conflict. If some members are ambivalent they can be perceived as not caring, which can hinder the group's development.

If ambiguous feedback is not clarified, the group will have difficulty stabilizing or getting anything accomplished because members won't know how to act or what is expected of them. By knowing how this process works, we can provide clear feedback during this time in the group's development to reduce uncertainty and establish ways of communicating to help the group accomplish its tasks.

Behavioral reinforcement can contribute to the social climate of the group. When positive behaviors of group members are met with positive feedback, it creates a social climate that makes the group attractive for its members fostering their commitment to the group.

This encourages communicating between members and motivates them to contribute for the good of the group. This also provides benefits by making members feel that they are valued and that they make a difference.

A positive climate can be developed by complementing one another, acknowledging other member's contributions to the group, agreeing with them, sharing credit for accomplishments, and recognizing their achievements. Supporting others can involve doing things for others as simple as offering someone a cup of coffee to helping them out when they need it.

If a member disagrees all the time or there is excessive negative behavioral reinforcement, it can create a climate that can discourage the other group members from contributing to the group. This can create feelings of tension, anxiety, and dissatisfaction. It can lessen a member's commitment to the group and the other members.

Group norms.

The process of behavioral reinforcement creates a set of normal standard operating procedures, called norms, for the group. Groups do this because the members have to work together to develop their own ways of doing things.

Norms refer to a group's normal pattern of behavior consisting of the shared expectations that members have for behavior in the group. They let members know what is expected of them and what they can expect from the others. They often include how group members communicate with one another, how they behave, and how they make decisions, solve problems, and resolve conflicts.

The way that group members first accomplish a task can set a precedent, which if repeated can establish a norm as part of their standard operating procedures. For example, how the group resolves their first conflict may be repeated when conflicts reoccur whether it was effective or not. Precedents work rather like first impressions. They may not be effective, but after they have been established, they can be difficult to change.

This is a process that happens naturally or it can be purposely managed. Precedents may be created haphazardly that can hinder the group's success making it difficult to change later on. It can be helpful to be aware of how this process works in order to create precedents early in the group's history that create positive norms to help the group achieve its desired outcomes.

In order to form a fully functioning group, norms need to be stabilized so that group members will share the same perceptions and expectations. They need to know what is expected of them and what they can expect from the other members. People don't like surprises or uncertainty, they want stability and predictability especially in others who are close to them and with whom they share a common purpose.

Without norms every group member would do whatever they felt like doing reducing the group to chaos so nothing would get done. Norms provide a means of establishing boundaries for behavior and structure so the group can accomplish its task.

Groups establish task norms based upon the needs and wants of the group. The purpose of task norms is to regulate the behavior of individuals so that the group can accomplish its tasks. These norms determine how individual group members work together in order to keep them on track to achieve their desired outcomes.

This can include procedures on how the group accomplishes its tasks such as setting priorities and establishing deadlines. Task norms can be used to determine the process of how decisions are made, problems are solved, and conflicts are resolved. They can determine how resources are allocated like how time and space are used.

Groups not only have task norms, they also have social norms. People do not just work together, they need to get along with one another. These norms regulate the social aspects of the group including how group members interact with one another. They determine who communicates with whom, about what, and under what circumstances. They can regulate how members communicate with others outside the group. They help to give meaning to the experiences of group members.

Groups often have a history and traditions that are shared between group members to provide a meaningful connection with the past. Social norms communicate how members participate in the activities of the group including rituals and traditions. These can include celebrating birthdays and holidays as well as informal rituals like getting together for coffee.

Group norms must be stable in order to provide structure for the group, however, groups also need the flexibility to change. As circumstances, tasks, and group members change, norms need a way to change as well. Groups need a mechanism to adopt new norms that are helpful and to discard those that are a hindrance.

By having an awareness of how this process works, members can choose to change their norms in a purposeful manner to become a more effective group, rather than waiting until circumstances force them to change.

Group roles.

Norms are the shared expectations that group members have of the group's behavior and roles are the shared expectations members have of each individual member. Groups have needs and wants that must be fulfilled, desired outcomes to be met, and tasks to be accomplished.

In order to accomplish them, someone has to do the work and who does what work comprises a role. A role is a specialized type of behavioral norm consisting of the perceptions and expectations that each member has about their individual duties and responsibilities in the group. Roles are based on the needs and wants of the group because this is how they are fulfilled.

A role in the group is rather like a role of an actor in a play or movie. Each actor knows what they and the other actors are going to do providing predictability enabling them to perform their role. Roles let group members know who is responsible for doing what tasks, so that each person can do their job and the group can function effectively.

Roles in groups can be developed through the process of behavioral reinforcement similar to how norms are established. Groups need to have things done and group members need to do them. Group members take on individual tasks and their actions are either accepted, rejected, or met with indifference by the other members. When the group approves of what a member does, the member will fill a role and when everyone has their role, the group's structure will stabilize.

If the group responds negatively or ignores a member's behavior, their role will not be established because it is not supported. It's helpful to have an awareness of how this process works to help stabilize roles, norms, and rules within the group as soon as feasible, so it can function effectively and get on to accomplishing its tasks.

In this process of determining roles, people do not necessarily choose their own role, but instead they negotiate for it with other members of the group. Without the support of other members a person cannot effectively fulfill their role. If more than one person tries to fulfill a role, there may be a conflict as they vie for the group's approval until one person is chosen.

When all members agree who is responsible for doing what tasks, the group structure will be established and the group can accomplish its tasks. If this does not happen, the group structure will not stabilize and things could become chaotic undermining its effectiveness.

While it is important for roles to be well defined in order for the group to function, groups need a mechanism to change roles within the group when necessary. Roles need to be changed in order to account for changing group members, circumstances, and tasks. There may be new duties and responsibilities that need to be allocated to existing members.

When a person joins the group, they need to find their place in the group. When a person leaves the group, the other members may need to pick up the slack. Clearly defined roles are important so that everyone knows who is responsible to do what tasks to avoid tension and conflict.

When a member joins or leaves the group or the task changes, the group may need to go through the process of behavior reinforcement again to renegotiate the roles within the group. This can happen even in established groups. If the group is aware of this process and how to utilize it, they can effectively renegotiate new roles in a positive way to get on with their work.

If they are unaware of it, this situation may cause unnecessary frustration with the group that can lead to increased dissatisfaction that may result in the loss of the member's commitment. This is how effective groups can become unproductive after a change in membership. It can also provide a means for getting the group going again if it has problems.

Norms and roles develop because a group has to establish certain behaviors and ways of communicating in order to fulfill its needs and wants, so it can accomplish its tasks. If everyone does whatever they want or if they all do the same thing, then the group will be in disarray increasing uncertainty.

The law of uncertainty motivates people to take action to reduce uncertainty, so group members will be motivated to reduce it by developing group norms and roles. The group has to reduce uncertainty in order to work effectively, so it can accomplish its tasks. It does this using a set of rules, which must be clearly communicated, so everyone knows what to expect.

Group rules.

In order for groups to function properly, there needs to be a mechanism to regulate behavior. That mechanism helps to establish the rules for the group. Where norms are shared expectations of group behavior and roles are shared expectations of individual behavior, rules are the shared expectations of how both are governed.

When a group first forms it may have no rules, so members might use rules from its members, other groups, or from a larger organization, if it is part of one. Even if the rules are established when the group first forms, there is often an informal process when the unwritten rules are established.

Rules are often created by the process of behavioral reinforcement, so members exhibit different behaviors that are either accepted or rejected by the other group members. Members try out different behaviors based upon their past experience and their perceptions of the needs and wants of the group. When a behavior is deemed acceptable by group members and is repeated over time, it can become part of the norms of the group.

For example, when the group first meets and someone wants to speak, they might raise their hand because they did so in a previous group. If others do the same and support that way of doing things, it can become part of the group's rules. However, if a behavior is rejected, it is not necessarily discarded like a norm or role, it may become part of the rules that this behavior is not accepted.

Rules regulate the behavior of group members. While this may seem restrictive, it is necessary in order to reduce uncertainty, create stability, and increase predictability so that group members can invest their resources in one another and in the group. Without rules no one would know what was expected of them and the group could not function.

Generally, the smaller the group, the more informal the rules. The larger the group, the greater the potential for disagreement or conflict, so more formal rules are often needed. Even when there are written rules there are often informal rules that govern everyday behavior that are usually not written down.

Members may consider informal rules as important as the formal ones. They may not be openly communicated, so members may not even know they exist until they break them.

Practically all aspects of our lives, all groups we belong to, and every endeavor we are involved in is governed by some set of rules. Rules do not just tell us what to do, they can also give us helpful advice how we should do things. They are meant to help us do things better and are often based on the experience of others.

Rules are necessary in order to create structure within groups and within society. For example, members of a musical group cannot play whatever they feel like playing.

They have to agree on the rules including what music to play, how to play their instruments, and how to perform together with others in a group. Groups need rules to function properly and to be effective by creating stability because everyone knows what to expect.

When a member joins a group they need to know the rules. Since some rules are not written down, new members learn them gradually from experience over time. It takes time to become adjusted to the norms of the group because all too often current members assume a newcomer will just get it.

The most common way a new member learns about the rules and norms of the group is by observing the behavior of others and emulating it. If they are not sure about something, they could ask existing members who may or may not tell them. Often newcomers only learn the rules and norms when they violate them and are punished by the group. To help new members understand the rules and norms, a longtime member could help them by providing advice and answering questions.

Group structure.

Groups need structure because it creates stability to reduce uncertainty. This provides predictability so that people can invest in the group and work together to accomplish its tasks. Structure is necessary for many aspects of the group including its roles, rules, norms, networks, and boundaries.

Smaller groups generally have less structure since everyone can communicate directly with everyone else. As groups grow in size, communicating between members becomes more difficult, so structure is needed for it to function effectively.

Having a formally recognized structure gives groups legitimacy by letting outsiders know who is responsible for what tasks. As a group becomes more formal, it may have more formal positions as part of its structure like president, CEO, secretary, or treasurer. These positions give the group legitimacy and creates the perception of professionalism and competence.

Groups not only have formal structure they also have informal structure. A formal structure is comprised of the ways in which group members are expected to interact with one another. This structure may not have been created by the group members themselves, but by other people outside the group such as a larger organization.

The informal structure often reflects how members actually communicate and their everyday behavior. As organizations become larger they need to develop structures to function effectively, but these can also serve as barriers to effective communicating. This can motivate members to utilize informal networks by making connections that get around the rules so that they can get things done.

Groups need structure, but they also need to adapt to changing circumstances. This creates tension between having a fixed structure and a need for flexibility. Highly structured groups tend to be less flexible reducing their adaptability to change with changing circumstances. Groups that are moderately structured provide for change within an established structure, but more serious change may be difficult. Flexible groups are able to change rather easily which may increase uncertainty.

A group needs to find its own degree of adaptability depending upon its needs and wants, the task to be accomplished, and how comfortable members are with change. For most groups an effective approach falls somewhere in the middle where there is a clear structure that is flexible enough to change as necessary.

However, there are groups that need to be more structured. This approach works because the objective is clear and the method to achieve it is well defined. Conversely, a more flexible structure can be effective for groups where creativity and developing new ideas are important to the group's success.

A flexible structure works well in areas like technology where groups need to adapt to new ideas and different styles quickly, but also needs structure to keep everyone organized.

Most businesses tend to be structured with clearly established norms that allows for some types of change, but it may resist others. When a group grows larger it needs to develop structures to help it function, but over time these structures can become overly bureaucratic or strict reducing flexibility and its ability to function effectively.

Group boundaries.

Boundaries are an integral part of a group's structure. They can be external, formed around the outside of the group and internal, existing within the group. External boundaries define who is a member and who is not by separating insiders from outsiders. They regulate who is allowed to participate in group activities, which gives members a feeling of being part of a group.

Boundaries have both positive and negative effects on a group. The stricter the boundaries the more difficult it can be for people to cross them, which can make a group more exclusive. Boundaries can restrict the flow of information coming in and out of the group. The more flexible the boundaries, the more information that can get into the group. However, members may feel less connected to other members.

Internal boundaries are often used within a group to regulate behavior. They can be used to create hierarchies, ranks, or levels of authority by giving some people more status and importance than others. This can provide motivation for members to stay with the group for longer periods of time, so they can move up the ranks to get more benefits.

Boundaries can be used to control the flow of information regulating who communicates with whom, about what, and under what circumstances. They can be used to create power within a group by restricting access to certain people. They can be used to help people work more effectively by grouping members together by profession or task, like having a sales team.

Not all boundaries are the same. They can be open or closed, and strict or flexible depending upon the needs of the group. External boundaries can be used to regulate how easy it is for people to become a member of the group. If a boundary is open then it's relatively easy to become a member and for members to communicate with outsiders.

If a boundary is closed, it may be difficult or impossible for someone to join the group or for outsiders to communicate with people inside the group. Flexible boundaries allow for people to move around as needed to accomplish the task. Strict boundaries don't allow as much movement and are often found in more formal groups or organizations such as defining departments within a company.

How boundaries are constructed can be a matter of degree and balance depending upon the needs and wants of the group. For instance, if the boundary is too large, too flexible, or to open it feels less like a group and more like a crowd of people.

If the boundary is too closed, too strict, or too small members can feel constrained or restricted possibly inhibiting them from accomplishing their task. Having a balance means having clear boundaries, while allowing the group to adapt to change as necessary.

Group networks.

Groups do not exist in isolation, they have connections with others outside the group. They are often a part of a larger organization as well as the larger community.

People do not communicate only with other group members, but also with people outside the group. Networks help regulate the perceptions and expectations of group members by letting them know how well they and the group are doing.

Members make connections outside the group because they may need resources the group does not have to fulfill their needs and wants. They need to gain information in order to make good decisions. The better the quality of the information a group has, the better decisions it should make. This can make the group more effective so members feel satisfied with the group increasing their commitment.

Networks are a series of connections between people that moves information in, out, and around a group. Groups create norms to manage their boundaries to maintain their group's integrity rather like countries use borders and customs to control what goes in and out of a country. In a group, not every member talks with every other member the same amount or in the same manner.

A network consists of who communicates with whom, under what circumstances, and about what topics. Networks help to fulfill group members need for information. How information flows in and out of the group can tell a lot about the group, its openness, its rules, its boundaries, and its structure.

Formal networks follow an established hierarchy carrying official information for the group or organization. Informal networks generally carry information that people are interested in and want to receive. Networks work because they follow the process of communicating by making connections between people. One person can serve as a liaison or gatekeeper to bring information into the group or keep information out.

The more connected a member is to other networks, the more information they are likely to have access to, which can give them more power within the group. Networks can form a chain that goes through the group or organization or they may look like a wheel with one person serving as the hub communicating with others as the spokes.

III. Group Maintenance, The Law of Investing Phase.

Once uncertainty has been reduced and group members share meaning to develop the group, they need to invest in the group and each other to maintain the group. Groups provide benefits, but they also require contributions from their members. These contributions can be in the form of time, energy, emotions, attention, and material things like money.

The perceptions and expectations members have of receiving benefits for contributions can affect their satisfaction with their group, their commitment to the group, and what they are willing to do for the group. This begins the law of investing phase of group development, which is necessary to maintain the group over time.

When a group stabilizes, uncertainty is reduced making it more predictable. This gives the group a greater chance of having longevity, which creates value because it motivates members to stay with the group longer to receive benefits. When people have a perception of receiving future benefits from the group, it gives them a reasonable expectation that they will see the investment they make now payoff in the future.

This can make the group more desirable to its members and encourage them to increase their commitment to the group making it more valuable to them and others. Increased value raises the group's status increasing member commitment. Groups often increase in status when more people are willing to do more to be a member.

Individual members invest in the group when they begin to identify with the group and see it as their own. They may refer to the group as "my group" or "our group."

This is an expression of their collective sense of ownership and pride in the group. When they introduce themselves to others outside the group, they may mention that they are members of the group. They may even define their self-concept and manage their identity based upon belonging to the group.

Group satisfaction.

Satisfaction represents the degree to which an individual member is happy with the group based upon their perceptions and expectations. It is often based upon how well they feel their expectations have been met and the extent to which their needs and wants have been fulfilled.

The more members feel that these are being met, the greater their satisfaction increasing their commitment to the group. They are likely to do more for the group because they will not want to lose their benefits.

All too often groups become more concerned with getting the task accomplished than with member satisfaction. If the group does not work well together or is not successful, members may wonder what happened.

Having awareness of the law of investing phase of group development enables leaders and members to increase group satisfaction without necessarily requiring more resources. The more individual members feel a sense of satisfaction, the more they will be committed to the group and willing to work for the good of the group to make it successful.

Groups and organizations may try to improve the quality and effectiveness of the group, however, when it doesn't work it can leave them wondering what went wrong. If members become dissatisfied with the group they are more likely to contribute less, be less committed, and the group will suffer.

If they are dissatisfied enough, they might compare their circumstances to other groups to see if they can get a better deal somewhere else. This can create a climate of dissatisfaction in the group undermining its effectiveness. If enough people become dissatisfied with the group it may deteriorate or fall apart.

Group satisfaction is often based on the perceptions and expectations of individual members. Everyone has expectations of what they want to contribute as well as receive from the groups they join. Most people expect to make fair contributions and receive fair rewards. These perceptions are usually based upon a person's past experiences and what they have received in the past. For instance, what some may consider generous monetary compensation others may see as inadequate.

Group satisfaction is often based upon how members feel their needs and wants are being fulfilled by the group. We join groups to fulfill needs and wants we cannot fulfill ourselves, which creates expectations about what we feel we should receive as a member of the group. When a member's perception matches or exceeds their expectations, it can increase their satisfaction with the group.

So, if members have the perception that their needs and wants are being reasonably fulfilled, they are more likely to contribute to the group increasing their satisfaction with the group. After all, if group members are getting their needs and wants fulfilled, why would they want to leave?

If group members feel that their needs and wants are not being fulfilled, they may be less likely to feel satisfaction with the group. If their perceptions are not meeting their expectations, it can motivate them to look at other groups to see if they can do better. This can create dissatisfaction eroding their commitment to the group. If they become dissatisfied enough they might leave the group.

Group members communicate with people outside the group such as customers, clients, friends, family, people in the larger organization, and the community. They may have their own perceptions and expectations about the group and its members, which can be a source of satisfaction or dissatisfaction. They can be a source of social benefits making group members feel good about the group.

People outside the group can form a loose knit network of their own based upon their connections to the group members. It can be helpful to the group's effectiveness to consider the influence that these people have on the group.

Members may not be aware of just how much influence these people may have on the group. Through the process of communicating, members receive feedback from outsiders that can affect the group's self-concept and how they see themselves.

It can be helpful for groups to be aware of how people outside the group can affect them. Group members don't get all their support, like their needs and wants fulfilled by the group itself. They often depend on others outside the group to fulfill them, which can give those who do influence in the group.

The support members get from their families can help improve their self-concept and feeling of satisfaction raising the collective self-esteem within the group. A group may have social events that include these people to keep them informed about the group and to learn more about their perceptions and expectations.

It is important to know how satisfied members are with the group. All too often member dissatisfaction goes unnoticed, ignored, or members keep it to themselves because they don't want to be characterized as a complainer or risk their investment.

Members who tell others that they are dissatisfied may be rejected by the group to discourage dissent in the group. If members feel they could lose their investment, they could withhold their problems with the group until it builds up to the point where they can no longer deal with the tension, creating conflict or they may quit.

Dissatisfaction can be reduced by encouraging group members to share their thoughts and feelings without the fear of rejection. Groups may not be in a position to offer more material benefits, however, it is relatively easy to offer social benefits such as acknowledgment, recognition, and respect to bolster members' self-concept.

Utilizing these methods are effective because agreement is one of the strongest means of supporting others, it affirms their value to the group. When our ideas are accepted by others it elevates our status with the group.

Group commitment.

Commitment involves how much individual group members put the good of the group above their own interests. They put group goals above their own. They are willing to stay with the group through difficult times and work through conflicts to resolve them. They put aside their own needs and wants for the good of the group.

Groups necessitate making a commitment not only to the group, but also to the other members of the group. They can have a strong commitment to a group even though they may not get along with the other members. Conversely, people may stay in a group they don't feel very strongly about, but they may feel connected to the other members.

For instance, this might happen in a company where members may not be satisfied with what they do, but they feel they are working with a great group of people. The level of commitment members have to a group can help or hurt its effectiveness. So, it is important for group members to support other members because they in turn would want their support.

Groups have different degrees of commitment ranging from very low to very high. The degree of commitment is contingent upon the nature of the group, the individuals involved, and the task to be accomplished. For many groups, after reaching a certain level of commitment, having more commitment is not necessarily better. Some groups do not need a high level of commitment to function effectively.

IV. Group Dissolution, Return to The Law of Uncertainty Phase

When a member leaves the group it can be difficult. If a group experiences a lot of members leaving, the remaining members may feel abandoned or rejected. This is because our self-concept is connected to the groups we belong to based on how the other members communicate with us.

Leaving a group or organization can be difficult because when we leave we often leave friendships behind, give up benefits, and make changes that increase uncertainty reducing stability and predictability. We may feel a sense of loss and even go through a period of mourning.

If we leave to join a new group, we will go through the process of behavior reinforcement all over again by getting used to a new set of norms, rules, and getting to know a new group of people.

People leave a group either because they choose to or because they have to. People may choose to leave groups because the group is no longer meeting their needs and wants, they are looking for a change, or the group has changed from what they expected.

People leave groups because they retire, move away, are fired, or they have to leave. We should expect to leave groups and to have other people leave the groups that we are in. While knowing that leaving groups is inevitable and unavoidable, it doesn't always make it any easier.

When people create or join groups they probably never considered how the group will end or that it will ever end at all. Not all groups last forever, eventually many come to an end for a wide variety of reasons. They may have accomplished their task, they may no longer be fulfilling the needs and wants of their members, or they may no longer be relevant.

The group may have lost its founder or members who were the driving force behind the group. Since groups are created for a purpose, the purpose it was created for may no longer exist and the group has simply run its course. In these circumstances the time may have come to disband the group.

Some groups may realize that their time has come to an end, while others may fight on against the odds. We spend a great deal of time with others in groups, so when it ends we can feel a loss in our lives. However, it may be better to intentionally end a group that has come to the end of the line rather than painfully trying to keep it going as it slowly dwindles away.

Groups have traditions and rituals that celebrate important events for the group and its members. When someone retires there is often a celebration to commemorate their accomplishments.

Instead of letting the group slowly wither away, the group members could have this kind of event to retire the group and bring it to a close. The event can be used to celebrate the accomplishments of the group and its members giving them closure by spending one last time together as a group.

Groups and Uncertainty

Some groups seem to get along and things go well, so we don't think much about them. Other times nothing seems to work leaving us feeling frustrated. Groups and organizations can utilize the laws of uncertainty, shared meaning, and investing as a methodological tool to help diagnose problems and find solutions to make them more effective.

By managing uncertainty, businesses and organizations can balance uncertainty with uncertainty reduction to provide stability, yet motivate effective behaviors to foster innovation and avoid becoming overly complacent. They can promote shared meaning to create a common culture and positive climate that fosters desirable attributes like commitment and member satisfaction.

Investing in people will help to make businesses and organizations more effective. These laws can be utilized to fulfill needs and wants, manage perceptions and expectations, and achieve your desired outcomes.

Managing Uncertainty

The success of any business or organization is about making connections with the public, as well as between people within the organization. Businesses that will be successful in the future are those that make these connections to reduce uncertainty for their customers and employees.

Doing this can be helpful because one thing that we know for sure about the future is that people will be motivated by uncertainty. Businesses and organizations can benefit from identifying sources of uncertainty, how it can affect their business, and how it can motivate people's behavior. Uncertainty can have a wide variety of implications, so businesses can benefit from planning for uncertainty as part of their future planning.

The last hundred and fifty years has seen more advancement in our quality of life than ever before in history. Society has made great advancements to reduce uncertainty, but has it also made us more vulnerable to the law of uncertainty?

Since much of human activity throughout history has been motivated by the law of uncertainty, the process of uncertainty reduction should have resulted in a significant decrease in the amount of uncertainty people experience. However, more recently people experienced greater uncertainty than ever before in history.

Perhaps it is because the more complicated our systems become, the more vulnerable they are to uncertainty. Perhaps we should be looking at building social institutions to foster independence and self-reliance in order to flow with uncertainty rather than try to control it.

Life is uncertain. The world can be chaotic. Throughout history, most of human activity has been motivated by uncertainty. The purpose of this book is to explore how uncertainty affects us and what we can do about it. It influences how we think and motivates our behavior. Uncertainty affects all of us and most everything in our lives.

In an increasingly interconnected world, how do we protect ourselves from the potential affects of increasing uncertainty? While we may never fully control or understand the nature of uncertainty one thing is certain, uncertainty will be a part of our lives now and in the future.

HH
Heather Hill

www.ingramcontent.com/pod-product-compliance
Lightning Source LLC
Chambersburg PA
CBHW020207200326
41521CB00005BA/280